Guide to mudlarking

By

Jenny Ridgwell

First published 2024
Jenny Ridgwell 2024

Artwork by David Smith

A catalogue record of this book is available from the British Library.
Jenny Ridgwell asserts the moral right to be identified as the author of this work.
All rights reserved. By payment of the required fees, you have been granted the non-exclusive, non-transferable right to access and read the text of this e-book on screen. No part of this text may be reproduced, transmitted, downloaded, decompiled or stored in any form or by any means without permission from the author.

Care should be taken when mudlarking on the Thames foreshore as it is a dangerous and hazardous area. You need a permit from the Port of London Authority to mudlark and search the foreshore in between the Thames Barrier and Teddington. Check the tide times before venturing out. Anyone going down to the foreshore does so at their own risk. Neither the author nor the publisher can accept responsibility for any harm, damage, loss or prosecution that may be claimed as a consequence, directly or indirectly, of the use or misuse of guidance given in this book.

To Isobel

Contents

Introduction	1
What is mudlarking?	3
Why mudlark on the Thames foreshore?	5
Why do people mudlark?	5
Top 10s of Mudlarking	11
My 10 favourite finds	11
10 things I'd like to find	14
10 tips on how to mudlark	15
10 things to wear and pack	17
10 special tips from experience	20
10 tips on how to be a great mudlark	21
10 old and rare finds found in the Thames	23
10 strangest Thames finds	24
10 hazards of mudlarking	25
The Facts	28
Help if someone falls in the water	28
Mudlark permits and rules	29
Mudlarking tours and guided walks	33
Best Thames mudlarking places	38
Do tides matter?	44
How to get down to the foreshore	47
Thames Beaches	50
Thames Barrier	51
All about finds	52
The Society of Thames Mudlarks	57

The British Museum	58
London Bridge	59
The Thames Ecology	61
What about pollution?	61
Wildlife and Ecology	64
Wild swimming in the Thames	66
Food and drink finds	68
Oysters	68
Sugar	70
Eels	71
Whales	73
Burgess's Anchovy Paste	74
London Dry Gin	76
Batey's Ginger Beer	79
Sacred and Mindful	81
Sacred Things in the Thames	81
Is mudlarking mindful?	84
Does mudlarking make people happy?	85
What will mudlarks find in 500 years?	86
Charts	87
London Places with mudlark exhibits	87
Finds from the Thames	88
Wildlife in the Thames	105
Useful Contacts	110
Places with food, drink and great river views	116
Thames places to visit	122
Thames Beaches	124
Glossary of mudlarking terms	126
Mudlarking books and Magazines	134

Tours and walks	137
Groups with Mudlark Tours	137
My favourite riverside walks	141
Wapping Walk	142
Rotherhithe Walk	148
Putney Bridge Walk	154
South Bank Walk	160
City of London Walk	166
Greenwich Pier Walk	173
My river walk to Deptford	176
Nearly there	180
My Daft Mudlark Awards	180
More thoughts from mudlarks	184
Acknowledgements	189

Poem inspired by Leisure, a poem by W.H. Davies

Ode to Mudlarking
What is this life if, full of care,
We have no time to stand and stare?
No time to go down to the shore
With mudlarks finding pots galore
And lots of treasure from the Thames
Some Roman coins and even gems
There's buckles, brooches, pipes and keys
And many times we're on our knees.
Top mudlarks find a pilgrim badge
And flinters boast an axe or adze.
I'd love to find a dry sea horse
Some sacred stuff, Doves font of course.
A poor life this if, full of care,
We mudlarks have no time to stare.

By Jenny Ridgwell

Mudlark

Introduction

Welcome to my book, A Guide to Mudlarking.
Why have I written this book? Moving to live in a flat overlooking the River Thames, I gazed down on people quietly plodding along the riverbank at low tide. One day, I skidded down the muddy slipway, wondering if I was entering a forbidden landscape, and interrupted a man on his peaceful meandering.

'What are you looking for?' I asked him.

He grunted, put his gloved hand into his pocket, and took out a beige flint.

'Neolithic arrowhead,' he said and offered it for me to hold.

'How do you know that?'

The flint had sharp, thin edges and he'd found it amongst thousands of flinty stones. He looked at me as if it was obvious why he knew, and I had met my first mudlark expert. He also recognised that I was a novice with no clue about the river's treasures and we've become mudlarking friends. He even gave me my favourite birthday gift – a small bag of clay pipes that he'd found.

'You'll need a permit if you are going to come down here' was his farewell advice, and that evening, I went online and purchased a three-year Thames Foreshore Permit from the Port of London Authority (PLA) just before they stopped issuing them. Lucky to be one of the last people before they changed the rules. My journey into the fascinating world of mudlarking had begun. I soon learned about the moon and river tides, wearing the right clothes and gloves, washing hands after searching and keeping safe on the foreshore.

Since then, friends and strangers have been captivated by the stories I tell of mudlarks and their finds. Over the months, I've discovered the best time to venture down to areas of the riverbank as I've explored different parts of historic London.

The community of mudlarks shares their incredible knowledge on Instagram, Facebook, X, and YouTube (#mudlark) and has helped me identify the odd things I find. Please enjoy and discover their online postings – it's a new and magical world out there!

'You will find what you are meant to find', one famous mudlark told me, and it's true. But there is also luck, opportunity, and skill, which I will share with you in this guide.

Most of the information is online in the public domain. Use the research sites to find out more. Mudlarks have given up valuable mudlarking time to talk to me when I know they are desperate to search for treasure while the tide is low, so thank you.

The Port of London Authority (PLA) decides who is allowed on the historic riverbank of the Thames, and you need a licence to mudlark. Otherwise, you can join the tour groups down onto the foreshore with expert leaders who tell you about the area's history and explain what you can find in the shingle and mud.

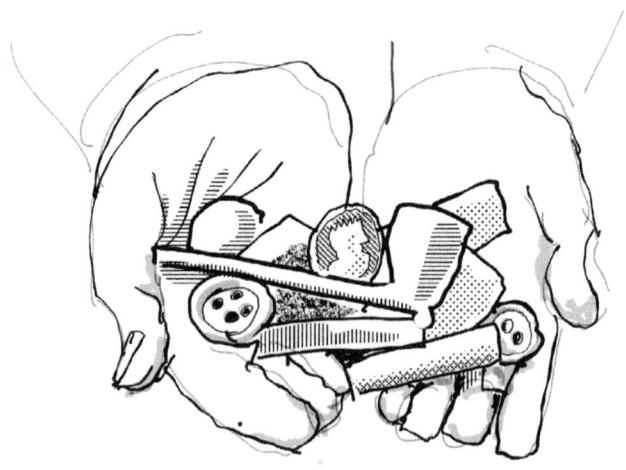

Handful of finds

Introduction

This book focuses on the Thames foreshore from Teddington to the Thames Barrier, an area administered by the Port of London Authority. East of the Thames Barrier, the river widens and the shoreline can be dangerous. Mudlarking is not permitted east of the Thames Barrier, including Tilbury and the Thames Estuary.

My previous work was writing school textbooks, so I've used those blunt and precise skills to create a factual reference for people interested in mudlarking. The stories, the finds, and the walks along the riverbank give me great pleasure. I like finding old and even modern things like the multicoloured disposable vapes, which sadly get thrown into the river after their smoking power has long gone. Maybe, in a hundred years, future mudlarks will pick them out of the water, learn their story and be amazed. They might find discarded NOS capsules and Cream Chargers, which dispense nitrous oxide gas for the riverbank party goers who need a giggle from the laughing gas they contain and discover their story too.

Gradually, I've awarded myself Mudlarking Level 2 as I've become more skilled, but I'm still attracted to weird and unusual finds. You can learn about my daft award system at the end of the book.

Thankyou to the river and the transformation that the mudlarking community has given me, bringing an awareness of stillness, tranquillity, and an appreciation of the small things of the past.

Jenny Ridgwell 2023

What is mudlarking?
In Victorian times, many of the poorest London people including children survived by mudlarking and scavenging in London's rivers and sewers, searching for things to sell. All sorts of finds could be traded, and mudlarks collected chunks of coal, took bones and discarded bits of metal to nearby rag shops and sold clay pipes, old

coins and bits of jewellery to local collectors. Many mudlarks worked in the busy areas where the barges were unloaded on the Thames and picked up things that were accidentally or even deliberately dropped into the river.

The writer Henry Mayhew (1812-1887) said of the mudlarks:

'They peer in the mud searching for coals, bits of old iron, rope, bones, and copper nails that drop from ships while lying or repairing along the shore.'

Today's mudlarks still search the riverbed for treasures, combing the Thames foreshore, which is accessible for a few hours a day at low tide, finding objects lost hundreds or even thousands of years ago as well as modern stuff like paper money, lost phones and jewellery.

Each person's idea of treasure is different. I'm attracted to sparkly, colourful things and I love the excitement of finding an old coin or button, especially if a story is attached to its history, but they are trickier for me to find. These days, we peer and search for pipes, pins, porcelain, and plastic! I've learnt that everything has a story.

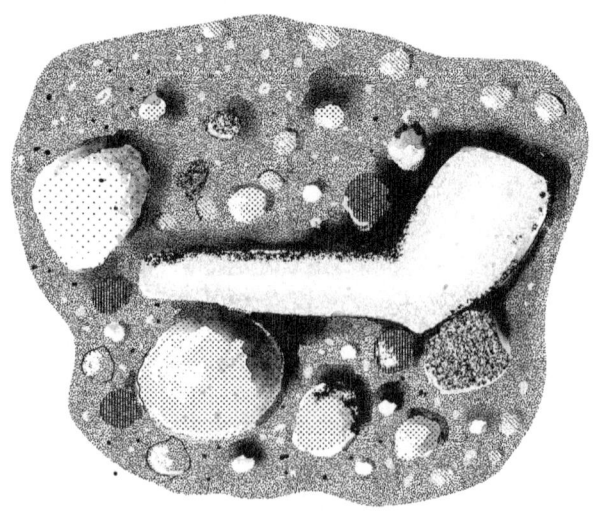

Clay pipe

Why mudlark on the Thames foreshore?

The River Thames has been London's dustbin for over 2,000 years. The history and location of London's river make the Thames a treasure trove for archaeologists, historians and mudlarks. In the 17th century, London was the largest port in the world. Many goods from around the globe came on ships to the City by river, uploaded onto barges and then taken to the wharves.

The people who lived along the river, starting with ancient people left their flint tools. Then came the Anglo Saxons making offerings to their gods to help them conquer new territories. The Romans came leaving coins, jewellery, hairpins and treasure near the foreshore. As London expanded, places were built, caught fire, demolished and rebuilt again, and the detritus from their homes and possessions often ended up in the river. So much trade took place, so many people travelled along the river, London was bombed in the Second World War, and stuff just accumulated and was washed away on the tides. Today, people lose their phones as they lean over on a riverboat cruise, bank notes float away in the wind, and ex-lovers toss unwanted engagement rings into the water for mudlarks to find. So, there will always be something to find on the Thames foreshore.

Why do people mudlark?

As I walk along the riverbank, I sometimes ask people why they mudlark.

Mudlarks have a limited time to search the shoreline at low tide, so their responses are much appreciated. These insights explore why mudlarking is such an enjoyable activity and why it's not just about finding valuable treasure.

Thankyou to the women, men and children who gave their answers.

So the question is, 'Why do you mudlark?'

Mudlark

'It's a time to stop. Stop being busy, relax and take time off from work.'

'It's mentally and physically challenging.'

'Finds make my brain ping.'

'It's the possibility of anything.'

'A quiet time away from stuff.'

'It's a place to reset. The foreshore is different from the rest of London. It's quiet and peaceful.'

'Finding history. I love it.'

'I like becoming an expert in the things that I'm passionate about.'

'It's a time to hyperfocus on finding things.'

'I'm relentlessly curious.'

'Tranquillity and peace. Thinking time alone.'

'It calms me down.'

'The tides remind us daily that things change, and yet they remain the same.'

'I love my time alone by the river.'

'It's real history that you can touch.'

'It gets me out of the house.'

'I love the endless change – the weather, the tide, the foreshore.'
'It engages my eyes and disconnects me from day-to-day things.'
'Expect the unexpected.'
'It's the only time my mind is truly quiet.'

'You stop thinking about your worries in this inspiring place, and you do things that make you excited.'

'I discovered the need to be beside the Thames. A place to be calm, to reflect, to clear the mind, to just 'be'. A place to connect with like-minded, open-hearted souls, the searchers of knowledge and often of themselves.'

Ted Sandling wrote this in his book, A Mudlark's Treasures – London in fragments.

'The Thames presents treasures with delightful serendipity: it gives up a hundred random objects, and it is up to the finder to discover their stories. That is the joy of mudlarking: after every trip to the river, you know more than you did before. Chance connections with something that was once treasured, that was once lost and has now been found again. Even the meanest broken fragments tell a story of this great city.'

Lucie Commans @luciecommans wrote,

'I'm a daydreamer, and the foreshore is the perfect place for me for contemplation, picking up objects and imagining stories of past Londoners. I believe that the river always gifts people with what I call 'river blessings', and it's always something personal.'

Nat @themerrymudlark discovered mudlarking when she moved to London 30 years ago. I met her on the foreshore when she'd found a piece of pilgrim badge.

'The reason why I mudlark and enjoy it is curiosity. Every find, from the smallest to the most exciting, leads to so much delving into new knowledge and so many new discoveries. It is probably the prime motivator topping all of the other great reasons – the meditative state one goes into, the community, and the direct link with history and the people of the past. So, yes, curiosity, and now I'm going to delve into the different kinds of 18th century paste gems and see what I can find out.'

Flint tool

Steve Crow is a flint expert whom I met on the foreshore:

'It helps with my ADHD as I'm calmer and less fidgety when I mudlark. I started twenty years ago and used to metal detect but gave up, and now it's eyes only. I enjoy finding flint tools. One of my first finds was a flint blade and when I found out its age and learnt it was Mesolithic or Neolithic, I was hooked.'

Steve has found flint tools that are in museums, and he recently discovered a 1st century Roman statuette of the goddess Venus, which was made from clay from the Rhine Valley. The Museum of London is currently evaluating it.

Tobias Nehmy Neto @tob2n is a mudlark who found the part of a Victoria Cross from 1854. See his story later on.

'Mudlarking is my past-time. It thrills me to unearth what Londoners of centuries past used and treasured.'

Joseph metal detects on the foreshore

'I started with eyes only seven years ago, and now I metal detect as well. It's real hands-on history where you touch things instead of looking at them in a case in a museum. I like the research and the stories when you start by not knowing what something is. I've recently found Roman coins and a Roman melon bead.'

Lewis (A teenager I met on the foreshore and gifted him a sherd of sugar cone).

'It's cool cos you learn lots about history that you've missed at school. It's fun to uncover history and get some exercise at the same time.'

In an article in The Times by Louise Eccles, the actor Gwendoline Christie from Game of Thrones describes her hobby of mudlarking.

'There's something secretly thrilling about unearthing slivers of artefacts, tokens of another age, further reaching through time to touch a connection with our ancestors.'

Wendy Fletcher is a professional archaeologist who travels to London to mudlark.

'I began collecting scraps of pottery and clay pipes when knee high to a grasshopper, hiding my treasures beneath a slab in the garden. I suspect they're still there! I went on to become a professional archaeologist but sadly had to give it up. I miss it terribly, but mudlarking goes a long way to scratching that itch.

It gives me a focus and a distraction from life's problems, and I can do as much or as little as my circumstances allow, safely and independently.

Always happiest outdoors, donning wellies and a tatty bumbag, dodging the boat wash whilst scrabbling around on my knees in the muck is for me therapeutic and hugely rewarding. Even the planning and anticipation of a trip to London (I live in Yorkshire) works wonders! I've met some lovely people, and you can't beat the thrill of seeing a Mesolithic flint blade or a Roman gaming token tumbling around in the water lapping at your feet.

The post-lark routine of cleaning, sorting and research throws up unexpected little surprises and keeps my inquisitive brain ticking over, as does reading and learning about fellow mudlarks' finds. 'Show and Tell' to family and friends adds another dimension that I thoroughly enjoy. I'd love to solve the mystery of the Thames garnets once and for all, and find a Bronze Age sword, obviously... Failing that, finding my first bone die would do!'

Sean Clark is an expert mudlark that you will meet at Mudlark exhibitions @seanclarkmudlark.

'I found Mudlarking after my beautiful wife, Trudy, passed away. Two reasons why I love Mudlarking. Firstly, the Thames foreshore is magical and so atmospheric. In such an iconic city once you walk down to the river you are walking on a tapestry of history. It is so beautiful and peaceful. Secondly, you start to find beautiful things and your journey of research begins. Who lost it? Who threw it away? What was their story? Mudlarking has changed my life!'

Top 10s of Mudlarking

My 10 favourite finds

These are some amazing things that I've found – they've opened my eyes to be curious, sent me on unexpected, investigative journeys, introduced me to knowledgeable, helpful people and shown me the wonders of mudlarking.

1. My best find is an ARP button (Air Raid Precautions) found on the shoreline on the day that Russia invaded Ukraine in 2022, which seems spooky. The person who wore this badge during World War 2 would have been a member of the civil defence team for wartime protection and probably helped people find underground shelters during the London bombing raids.
2. An echinoid fossil is my oldest find – a sea urchin that lived between 35 and 100 million years ago. I now have five in my collection. It seems they were brought in as ballast for the sailing ships and with the lumps of chalk that you'll find in areas on the riverbank where the barges were loaded and unloaded. Sharp shingle and stones on the foreshore could damage the barge hulls, and a chalk bed made for a softer landing.
3. My most important find is my first clay pipe. It has no monetary value, but it opened up the fascinating world of mudlarking, discovering their dates and designs and the stories of their decorations.

4. A tiny red and black trade bead was given to me by a lady mudlark when I was sitting on the sand, feeling glum, unsuccessful and unskilled at not finding things. It was a gift of kindness and a deep dive into how we built an empire selling and trading goods and people.
5. Two old bones, each with a diagonal cut at one end and a small hole near the blunt end. I posted a photograph on Facebook and asked, 'What were these used for?' which received nearly 100 replies. The answer? Who knows? A back scratcher, a useful tool, a pinner's bone, a weaving tool, a scraping tool, and finally, someone posted a photograph of an exhibit in Clink Prison describing it as an apple corer. It taught me that the identity of things collected from the river can be a mystery, and the stories are fascinating.

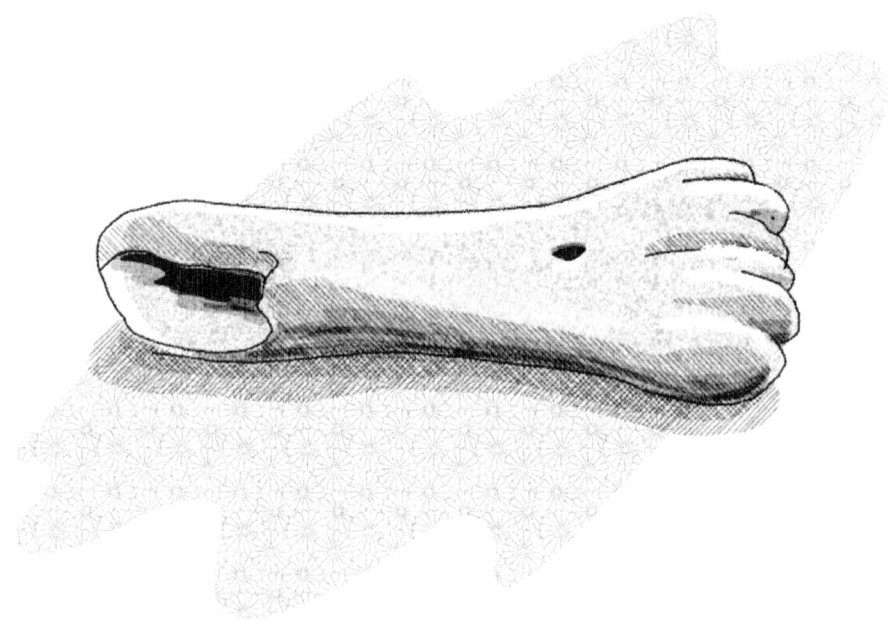

Bone tool

6. The knop of a green-glazed, ceramic Tudor money box used in the theatres on the Southbank in the 16th century to collect performance takings. The top (knop) had to be broken off the pot to count the money, and Tudor litter louts must have thrown my knop in the river.
7. A pewter medallion celebrating Queen Victoria's Coronation on June 28 1838, when she was just twenty years old and had her hair tied up in a tight bun. It's a bit chipped after I soaked it in vinegar and scrubbed it, which I now know was a stupid thing to do. This medallion was one of many made and must have been great PR for the young queen and her team and a start of things to come.
8. A pottery head of the Hindu God, Ganesh, is part of a larger statue that was probably thrown as an offering into the river and smashed into pieces. Lord Ganesha clears obstacles and helps us move forward, so let's hope for great things in the future for all of us. My Ganesh has beautiful brown eyes, a red Trishul mark on his forehead, decorated earrings and an elaborate headdress. Should I have fished it out of the river? The Hindu community thought this was OK and would bring me good fortune.
9. The lid of a pot of Burgess's Anchovy paste, a Victorian delicacy from The Original Sauce Warehouse 107 Strand Corner of the Savoy Steps London. It's 19th century, black transferware showing a Royal Warrant and Queen Victoria's crown. You can read its story later on.
10. A broken jar of Dundee Marmalade, a company that was first in so many things. They created the first commercial marmalade brand and opened the world's first marmalade factory in 1797. When the British Trademark Registry Act came into force in 1876, Keiller's Dundee Orange Marmalade was one of the first brands to be registered. A clever business model.

Dundee Marmalade

10 things I'd like to find

1. A piece of Doves Press typeface
2. An intact clay pipe with a complete bowl and pipe stem
3. A pilgrim's badge – from a pilgrimage from anywhere
4. A whole torpedo glass bottle
5. An intact Frozen Charlotte
6. A wig curler from the 17th century
7. A flint axe head
8. The top of a Bellarmine jug with the entire face
9. A dried seahorse
10. An old coin of some sort from Roman times.

See Chart on Finds from the Thames for details.

Bellarmine Jug

10 tips on how to mudlark

These tips have come from talking to and watching some of the best Thames mudlarks.

1. You need a licence from the Port of London Authority (PLA), with a permit to mudlark. See Mudlark Permits for more details.
2. Get down to the foreshore early, before low tide. Things wash up as the water recedes, and sometimes, a treasure waits for you on the newly exposed shingle. One mudlark found a 14th

century pilgrim badge lying on stones just as the tide turned. The River God was giving her a blessing that day.
3. Check the Thames Tide Table for tide times and find the special low tides that expose greater areas of the foreshore. Watch the incoming tide as you lark – there's the danger of getting trapped by the river as the water rises. Tell someone if you're mudlarking in a new area and you don't know that foreshore well.
4. Dress ready for wet, cold or hot weather so you can stay on the foreshore as long as the low tide allows. Wear waterproof boots, a waist pouch, and gloves, and carry a rucksack.

Wear waterproof boots

5. Take a well-charged mobile phone – it's useful in emergencies to get help if you or someone else is trapped or injured on the foreshore. You can use your phone to film and photograph your finds, and people are impressed when you take photos 'in situ' on the foreshore.
6. Never give up searching – history is under your nose, so be confident, watch, look, and enjoy. At the end of your search, something can suddenly appear.

7. Take your time – successful mudlarks don't speed along. They stand still like the river herons, peering into the water, looking down at the shingle, and scanning the foreshore. Crouch down, kneel, and slowly search. You'll see things others have missed. Not everyone spots things like you or is interested in what you like to find. Stroll along the foreshore, looking at the ground slowly from side to side. See what attracts your attention and interests you. You'll walk over shingle, shells, building materials, glass and pottery and learn to find things like pipe bowls, pins and even coins.
8. Join the Mudlarking community on Facebook, Instagram and X. Make friends with other mudlarks. They may like to mudlark quietly, alone, but as you visit the foreshore more frequently, you may become part of this special group. Learn from these experts. They can help identify your findings, and in return, you can follow them on Instagram and Facebook.
9. You spend hours bending over as you mudlark, so every so often, straighten up to avoid aches and pains. When you get home, lie flat on the floor for a few minutes to straighten out.
10. Wash your hands thoroughly with soap and water after you remove your gloves to clean off river grime and before touching your face and eating and drinking. Clean your treasures in soapy water.

10 things to wear and pack

1. Waterproof footwear – choose sturdy boots or Wellington boots, which help you grip slippery, wet, and muddy steps and stones. No open-toed sandals. Take spare shoes in case your boots get wet and muddy or, like me, a wave from the riverboats washes over you and fills your boots with water.

Glass bottles

2. Wear casual clothes and choose layers, as the foreshore can be windy and feel colder than the street temperature, and the weather can change unexpectedly. Long trousers and long-sleeved tops protect you from the strong sun and save some injury if you trip over slimy stones.
3. Take a foldaway waterproof jacket for when it unexpectedly turns windy or rainy, as it is useful when you're on your knees on an intensive search and a downpour starts, yet you want to continue to mudlark.
4. Waterproof gloves like gardening gloves or disposable medical gloves protect your hands from dirty river water and mud. Medical gloves can tear if you handle sharp flints and broken bits, but they are easier to use if you want to use your phone to take photos and videos as you mudlark. It's trickier to film on your phone using thicker gloves. After you remove your gloves, wash your hands with hand sanitiser or soap and water.
5. Wear a hat, sunglasses and sun cream in summertime, especially on sunny and windy days. The glare from the river can be fierce, and my face has been burnt on several dull-looking days when the sun didn't seem to shine.

6. Pack a backpack with a water bottle, hand sanitiser, antibacterial wipes, small plastic bags, a small plastic box or tin for treasures, and a carrier bag if you litter pick.
7. A pouch strapped to your waist with zipped-up pockets is great for storing larger things like pottery sherds and saves time instead of opening your backpack.
8. Take a fully charged mobile phone for emergencies, photography and videos.
9. Tools like a small pointed trowel, a hand rake for scraping the shingle, and even tweezers are useful for picking up tiny things like garnets and beads if you are lucky! Remember, they can't be used in certain parts of the foreshore. If you want to look closely and identify small finds like Roman coins, a hand lens or magnifier is useful. In restricted areas with eyes only searching, you can't use trowels and rakes – you just look and pick up what you find.
10. Experienced mudlarks use a head torch for nightlarking, knee pads for kneeling on the shingle, and carry a bucket if they take muddy things home to clean up and research later.

Nightlark

10 special tips from experience

These are special things that I've learned from my mudlarking experiences.

1. Take a trip on the Uber Boat up and down the river from Putney to Woolwich. If you travel when the foreshore is exposed at low tide, you can spot the access points with stairs and slipways down to the river and look out for the wider areas of the foreshore, which are good for searching if you have not got your tide times correct.
2. Go to the Mudlark exhibitions held in Southwark Cathedral, St. Pauls, The Guildhall, The National Maritime Museum, and The Museum of London Docklands. Expert mudlarks display their finds and share stories, and there are specialist talks.
3. Research different areas of the river and discover their history. Older areas of the riverbank where people lived, traded and made river crossings may have some of the older finds like buckles, buttons and beads. Don't dismiss areas further from the City, like Putney and Hammersmith, where you can find interesting, modern finds like offerings and vapes and sometimes really old finds like Roman stuff.
4. Wear some waterproof knee pads if you are bending down on the shingle. When I slipped on some wet granite rocks, I fell on my kneepads and prevented injury.
5. Watch how other people search. Model excellence. Learn how to get your eye in and trained to spot things. For example, I love finding pins, but I was taught to crouch, kneel, or sit on the ground and take my time to look slowly and carefully. What emerges when you stare at the shingle is surprising.
6. You must travel along stretches of the riverbank to spot your larking sites and notice where people are searching. Locations are not usually shared online.

7. Buy a pot with a screw-on lid or a clip-lock box to store your tiny finds so they don't get lost. Small plastic sealable bags are great for the extraordinary stuff. A tiny gold coin slipped from my pouch back onto the riverbank as I hadn't packed it away safely.
8. Learn how to clean your finds. There's plenty of help online. And yes, I did it incorrectly and damaged a medallion by soaking it in vinegar and scrubbing it with a wire brush.
9. Watch the mudlarking posts on Facebook and Instagram – many knowledgeable people write about the detailed history of their finds, and you can learn so much.
10. 'You'll find what you are meant to find' was said to me by a famous mudlark. The river has much to offer, so enjoy the fresh air, the river traffic, the birds, the other mudlarks and the peace, even if you find nothing.

10 tips on how to be a great mudlark
This advice comes from mudlarks who have years of experience visiting the foreshore and have discovered real treasure.

1. Persistence, persistence, persistence. Great mudlarks spend a lot of time larking and don't give up searching until they climb off the foreshore.
2. Share your special finds with other experts who help identify the history of what you have discovered and often show you their finds in return.
3. Get your eye in – notice metal lines where nails, bolts and metal bits gather and learn how to spot round things like coins, tokens, and rings. If you want to find flint tools, focus on only looking at flints and don't get distracted. It's a skill I have not mastered yet.

4. The river is like a washing machine, churning and swilling things around. Explore different foreshore areas, observe how the shoreline erodes and notice where special things get washed up, as they often turn up there again.
5. Do your research. Follow Mudlarks on Instagram, Facebook groups and YouTube and start your own account and pages to share and discover more about your findings. Beginners are very welcome online, and people who just want to watch, admire and dream of one day joining in.
6. Visit the exhibitions, and if you have a collection of interesting finds, offer to help, display your finds or suggest an activity table that you can set up for visitors. Children especially enjoy these events. Mudlarks are keen to share, and visitors often bring things to identify.
7. Research online sites – the collections of The British Museum, The Museum of London, The London Archaeological Archive, and The Port and River Archive, to learn the stories of river finds.
8. Perseverance and patience – whatever the weather or time of year, great mudlarks visit the foreshore – rain or shine.
9. Mudlarks don't often disclose where they discover special finds, as others can visit and search there. An expert mudlark found some coins, kept quiet, and then returned months later and found some more. He called it his Hot Patch.
10. A metal detector is useful for finding tiny coins and tokens buried in the riverbank but is not used by many mudlarks in the central London area as it is forbidden.

Extra Note – Some mudlarks wear a Thames Mudlark badge with images of a skull and trowel. Sean O'Mara designed it, the number 346 on the badge is the length of the Thames in kilometres, and the line on the forehead of the skull shows the course of the river in central London.

Mudlark Badge by Sean O'Mara

10 old and rare finds found in the Thames

1. A 5,000-year-old human femur bone, analysed by scientists and dated between 3516 and 3365 BCE, will be used to research Stone Age people.
2. Roman artefacts such as coins, pottery, and statues date back to the Roman occupation of Britain in the 1st and 2nd centuries, which are 2000 years old.
3. A Mesolithic flint tool was found near Vauxhall Bridge in the 1970s. The tool is around 9,000 years old and shows evidence of early human activity.

4. The Battersea Shield made 350-50 BCE dredged from the Thames in 1857 during the construction of Chelsea Bridge. It may have been an offering and is now on display in the British Museum.
5. A double-horned Iron Age helmet called The Waterloo Bridge Helmet was found in 1868 by Waterloo Bridge. This ceremonial piece is also on display in the British Museum.
6. The bronze head of Emperor Hadrian was found near London Bridge in 1848, and is on display in the British Museum.
7. A 2000-year-old Roman bone hairpin. One is on display in St Bride's Church, Fleet St along with other Roman artefacts.
8. A well-preserved Medieval leather boot, thought to be over 500 years old.
9. A Tudor gold finger ring with a large cabochon ruby.
10. A rare 16th century gold posy ring with a secret message.

Finds in the river

10 strangest Thames finds

These finds were recovered from the Thames foreshore. Why and how did they end up in the river?

1. False teeth for the lower jaw, carved from hippopotamus ivory, made for someone wealthy.
2. In 1995, a giant Michael Jackson statue was found floating down the Thames. Experts think the singer used the statue to promote his album 'HIStory'.
3. A gold engagement ring with five large diamonds.
4. Tobias Neto, a metal detectorist, found an 1854 Victoria Cross medal, now in the National Army Museum. See his story further on.
5. 17th century gold memento mori ring – a mourning ring remembering the dead.
6. Medieval pilgrim badges, which pilgrims bought as souvenirs to add to their clothing or hats after a pilgrimage to a holy shrine.
7. In 2009, an iron ball and chain, used to shackle prisoners to prevent them from escaping were unearthed from the river bed,
8. Guns, explosives, bullet cases, and ammunition from the Second World War and weapons from recent times.
9. A 'river egg', one of several mysterious, egg-shaped objects discovered on the riverbank, each stamped with a number and 'London'. An anonymous artist, Anon, created 5,000 stoneware eggs in 2012 and then put the eggs in the river.
10. My strangest find – a large, purple dildo resting on the shingle in east London.

10 hazards of mudlarking

1. The river tides and the current are major hazards. Make sure you know how to get off the river when the water rises.
2. People and organisations throw all sorts of stuff into the river – raw sewage, bottles and glasses, and weapons such

as knives and guns. Be careful what you touch. Contact the police if you find weapons.
3. Steps and stairs down to the foreshore can be slippery and are not always well maintained. Check before you go down to the river.
4. Paddling in deeper parts of the river is dangerous, especially near inlets, so take care when going onto or leaving the foreshore.
5. Wear sturdy boots and waterproof gloves to protect yourself when mudlarking from sharp pottery pieces, rusty nails, metal spikes, broken bottles and hypodermic needles.
6. Don't pick up the pieces of asbestos on the foreshore near demolished buildings. Asbestos fibres are microscopic, and extensive exposure causes lung cancer.
7. Weil's disease is spread by rat urine in the water. Infection can be through the eyes, mouth or nose or cuts in the skin. Seek medical advice if you get flu-like symptoms, including a high temperature and aching muscles and joints, for up to two weeks after visiting the foreshore.

Mudlarking on the shore

8. Don't touch your face, mouth or eyes until you have washed your hands after searching on the foreshore.
9. Take spare dry clothes and shoes wrapped in a waterproof bag if you fall in the river or if a wave from a passing boat washes over you. That's a hazard I've experienced.
10. Muddy areas can be dangerous as you can sink into deep mud and get stuck. Check the safety of parts of the foreshore with other mudlarks and try not to go alone in these areas. I've sunk into deep mud once and it was a scary experience.

Danger on the foreshore – this information is provided by the Port of London Authority (PLA):-

'The Thames foreshore is a potentially hazardous environment that must be respected and contains some dangers that may not always be immediately apparent. The Thames can rise and fall by over 7 metres twice daily as the tide comes in and out. The current is fast, and the water is cold. Anyone accessing the foreshore does so entirely at their own risk. Individuals must take personal responsibility for their safety and that of anyone with them. In addition to the tide and current, other less obvious hazards can be encountered, including raw sewage, broken glass, hypodermic needles, and wash from vessels. Steps and stairs down to the foreshore can be slippery and dangerous and are not always maintained. Caution must be exercised when going onto or leaving the foreshore.'

The Facts

Help if someone falls in the water
If you see someone in trouble in the water, call 999 or 112 and ask for the London Fire Brigade, Coastguard or Thames River Police. They are quick in their response and travel by fast boats along the river. The London Fire Brigade has ten water rescue specialist units across the city and two fireboats at the Lambeth River Station.

The London Coastguard works alongside the Port of London Authority (PLA) at the London Maritime Rescue Sub-Coordination Centre (MRSC) to watch the river.
    There are four Royal National Lifeboat Institute (RNLI) stations – Tower, Chiswick, Gravesend, and Teddington – three of which have full-time staff members to handle the number of incidents they must respond to.
    Senior Maritime Operations Officer Paul said this about the Thames –
    'It's fast, and it's like a washing machine, and you will likely be pulled under very quickly. So our main focus is on a quick response – if you can't get there fast, the outcome is almost inevitably tragic.'
    I often see the orange boats of the Coastguard speeding along the Thames. In an emergency, they seem to fly through the water, James Bond style, on their way to help someone in trouble.

Thames River Police Marine Policing Unit MPU
The Thames River Police were formed in 1798 to tackle theft and looting from ships anchored in the Pool of London and the docks.

The MPU is responsible for policing 47 miles of the River Thames in London between Dartford and Hampton Court and responds to over 250 miles of waterways and lakes, reservoirs and canals across the rest of London.

They work closely with The Royal National Lifeboat Institute (RNLI), The London Fire Brigade, The Port of London Authority, The UK Coastguard, The London Ambulance Service, The Canal and River Trust and The Environment Agency. During emergencies, the Fire, Coastguard, and Police boats speed down the river to the rescue, so the Thames is actively patrolled for everyone's safety.

Thames Foreshore Permit

- Don't go into the water if someone else is in trouble – call the London Fire Brigade or the Coastguard.
- Never drink alcohol and then go for a swim or attempt to jump into the water.
- If you or someone else falls into the Thames, don't try to swim straight away. Relax and float on your back to catch

your breath. Get hold of something that will help you float. Keep calm, then call for help or swim to safety if you can.
- If you see someone in the water, dial 999 or 112 and ask for the London Fire Brigade, Coastguard or Thames River Police. They are quick in their response.
- Try to get an exact location if someone is in the river – use your phone to help. Throw a lifebuoy or a throwline to them if available. Don't go into the dangerous water yourself.

Mudlark permits and rules

The Port of London Authority (PLA) website states that from April 2023, new mudlarking permits were stopped. People with an existing permit can renew. The PLA administers the entire Thames foreshore from Teddington to the Thames Barrier on behalf of the Crown Estate as the landowner.

'Walking and searching on the Thames foreshore requires a permit to legally mudlark. New foreshore permits are not currently available anywhere on the foreshore from Teddington to the Thames Barrier. Searching includes searching by eye, metal detecting, digging, or scraping.'

Questions and Answers

1. Q. Can I visit the Thames foreshore without a permit?
   A. You can visit the foreshore but you can't search without a permit.

   This information is from The Port of London Authority (PLA) website in April 2023.

   'While you may visit the foreshore, you may not search the tidal Thames foreshore from Teddington to the Thames Barrier 'in any way for any reason' without a permit.' This includes all searching, metal detecting, 'beachcombing', scraping and digging.

The Museum of London and Historic England wants to preserve the 'delicate historical site which has come under increasing pressure from visitors'.'

2. Q. Can tourists mudlark?
   A. If you have a permit, yes. If not, join a licensed tour group. See the end for more details.

3. Q. Can I go metal detecting on the foreshore?
   A. Yes, in certain areas, if you have a permit. See the end for more details.

4. Q. Where can't I mudlark?
   A. The PLA map of the Thames shows restricted areas and sites of Scheduled Ancient Monuments where you can't mudlark. See the end for more details.

5. Q. Can I mudlark east of the Thames Barrier?
   A. No. According to the Port of London Authority (PLA), from 2023, mudlarking is banned east of the Barrier, including Tilbury and the Thames Estuary.

This ban is to:

- protect fragile ecological and wildlife habitats and archaeological sites,
- reduce complex emergency services callouts in a more dangerous foreshore environment than central London.

These rules focus on mudlarking in areas of the river foreshore administered by the Port of London Authority (PLA) from Teddington to the Thames Barrier. Beyond that, mudlarking is banned for people with and without licences.

Thames Path

Travelling along the Thames
The Thames Path London section covers 64 km (40 miles) with easy, level walking on both sides of the river from Hampton Court Palace, through the heart of London to the East India Dock Basin on the North Bank and the Royal Greenwich on the South Bank. The route is well marked by the National Trail symbol (an acorn) from the west of London to the end of the National Trail at the Thames Barrier in the London Borough of Greenwich (on the south side) and at Island Gardens (on the north side).

Uber Boats by Thames Clippers run services from early morning until late evening. Five River Bus routes operate from 20 piers between Putney and Woolwich, where the Woolwich Ferry crosses the river between Woolwich and North Woolwich.

Can I walk under the Thames?
Yes. If you want to walk under the Thames, there are two tunnels. The Greenwich Foot Tunnel was built in 1902, and The Woolwich Foot Tunnel was built in 1912. Both tunnels make an exciting walk as part of the river's history, provide access to mudlarking sites, and are open 24 hours a day if you fancy a bit of nightlarking.

The purpose of the tunnels was to provide reliable all-weather access for residents to cross to the London shipyards and docks on the north side of the Thames. Today, these tunnels are busy with people and their bikes, walking or cycling under the river, and used by around 1.2 million people in Greenwich and 300,000 people in Woolwich a year.

The Greenwich Foot Tunnel is an underground, tiled walkway which connects Greenwich Pier to The Isle of Dogs, linking the Cutty Sark to Island Gardens and Tower Hamlets. It's about a 10 minute walk under the river. There are stairs and lifts at each entrance, but sometimes the lifts are out of order, and getting up and down can be a trudge.

The Woolwich Foot Tunnel links Woolwich to North Woolwich, and the walk through takes around 15 minutes, with stairs and lifts at each entrance. The Royal Arsenal was the former site of one of the biggest munition factories in the UK, so there may be lost musket and cannon balls in the river nearby.

Ferries across the river
A cross-river shuttle operates between Greenland (Surrey Quays) Pier and Canary Wharf, which is useful if you are travelling by Uber Boat and need to cross from the north to the south bank or return.

Mudlarking tours and guided walks
These groups run popular tours – useful if you don't have a licence to mudlark. You need to book online.

- Thames Explorer Trust
- Thames Discovery Programme
- Thames Festival Trust
- Southwark Cathedral Walks – River Thames Foreshore Walks
- Meetup Group, London Culture Seekers.

To organise your group walk or guided tour, which will not incur disturbance of the Thames foreshore, apply for written permission from the Port of London Authority's Estates Department by contacting estates3@pla.co.uk. If the group activity involves any disturbance of the foreshore, each person must have their own Thames Foreshore Permit, and the event organiser needs permission from the Estates Department.

The walk information is based on 2023 guided tours from the Thames Explorer Trust, the Thames Discovery Programme and the Thames Festival Trust.

Thames Explorer Trust
'TET runs archaeology-guided tours along the Thames riverbank with experienced staff who will help you find and identify artefacts found on the foreshore.

Money generated from these events goes into supporting their work with schools. Thames Explorer requests visitors take only memories and photographs away and not artefacts.'

These are 4 of their walks.

1. Millennium Bridge – Start at the Millennium Bridge, on the North Bank, and explore the foreshore from the bridge to Queenhithe Dock. You may find smoking pipes, drainpipes, pottery, bones, Tudor roof tiles and bricks, and even pieces of Roman pottery.
2. Rotherhithe – Start at Brunel Museum, Railway Ave, and take stone steps to the foreshore.

3. Wapping – Start at the River View Chinese restaurant at 1 New Crane Place, London, and go down the steps to the foreshore.
4. Limehouse – Start at the Yurt Café in the grounds of The Royal Foundation of St Katharine, and walk to the stone steps leading to the foreshore.

Thames Discovery Programme (TDP)
These are some of the walks taken by one of their expert archaeologists to discover areas of the Thames foreshore. TDP provides volunteer training for foreshore archaeology recording.

'With permission from the Port of London Authority, some surface-only artefact handling may be permitted when attending a TDP foreshore walk. All finds must be examined by the archaeologist on site, and significant artefacts recorded with the Portable Antiquities Scheme.'

The Angel Pub Rotherhithe

These are 6 of their walks with their descriptions

1. Greenwich
   Starts at the Old Royal Naval College with easy access to the foreshore. Learn about Henry VIII's favourite palace in Greenwich and how it became a retirement home for naval sailors and then a college for training naval officers. Find out about the care of the poor in nearby almshouses and see the structures used to maintain boats and ships.
2. Wapping
   Starts at the river stairs next to the Town of Ramsgate Pub in Wapping. Learn about the oldest operational police station in Britain and the history of the river police. Find out about the history of crime and punishment in this area.
3. Rotherhithe
   Starts at Rotherhithe Overground Station. The walk explores how Rotherhithe became a centre of shipbreaking during the 19th century and finishes at Surrey Docks Farm.
4. Bankside foreshore
   Starts at the top of the River stairs next to the Founders Arms Pub. Learn about how an area of marshes and islands became the entertainment centre of Tudor London. Seek out evidence of 19th century industry. Find out about public transport on the Thames in days gone by.
5. Deptford's forgotten Shipbuilders walk
   Starts under the bowsprit at the front of the Cutty Sark, Greenwich. Discover Deptford's shipbuilding history, Henry VIII's dockyard and the private shipyards of the 19th century, almost three hundred years of maritime heritage. The walk finishes by South Dock in Rotherhithe.
6. Fulham Palace
   Starts at the top of the River Stairs in Bishops Park near to Putney Bridge. Learn about the wealth and power of the Bishops of London. Seek out evidence of Iron Age activity on

the foreshore. Find why a bridge was built here and what the first bridge was like.

Thames Festival Trust
The Trust celebrates the River Thames with arts events, active adventures, environmental initiatives, and heritage and education programmes.

These are 3 of their walks with their descriptions

1. Along the North Bank – explore the foreshore from Millennium Bridge to Southwark Bridge. During the tour, you can only take photographs, knowledge and memories, but not the artefacts themselves.
2. Bankside River Stairs, The Founders Arms.
3. Explore the archaeology of the Thames foreshore from Bankside to Gabriel's Wharf. See archaeology of the Southwark foreshore from its Roman origins to the 20th century. Explore the development of this area from tidal marshes and islands to an entertainment zone, to an industrial area, and back to a place of leisure.
4. Rotherhithe from Bermondsey Tube Station and ending at The Mayflower Pub. 400 years ago, the Pilgrims sailed from here when it was a small village in central London and later it became an East India Company town. Buildings were built from a shipwreck, and there's a Church with masts for pillars and chairs carved from ships. You'll see a Pirate's Gibbet, The Watch House, which guards the graveyard, a memorial to Christopher Jones, Captain of the Mayflower, and another to Prince Lee Boo, a hero from the Spice Islands.

Southwark Cathedral Walks – River Thames Foreshore Walks
   This is their description.

'Thames archaeologist Mike Webber guides a walk along the foreshore. Learn about London's past, how the Thames has shaped the history of this great City and how the lives of Londoners and visitors have mingled with the Thames for thousands of years. Start at Southwark Cathedral before walking either west alongside Bankside or over London Bridge to the City of London, where the foreshore walk will begin. You will be on the foreshore for 1.5 – 2 hours. Only those with a special permit issued by the Port of London Authority (PLA) can take objects found on the foreshore.'

Best Thames mudlarking places

Twice a day, when the tide goes out, you can get down to sandy, shingly, and muddy stretches of the foreshore and search for things which have been lost or dumped in the river over thousands of years. At first, I thought the areas near the City, where most people lived years ago, would have the oldest finds, but I've learnt that old and interesting things can be found all along the riverbank, so venture out into different places and try your luck.

You find many mudlarks gathered around the North and South Bank near London Bridge, which for hundreds of years was the main river crossing, and some interesting discoveries have been made there, including pilgrim badges, all kinds of old coins, buckles, buttons and beads. Check out The British Museum's website for their Collections as they list the items found in this area and describe where they were found.

Google Earth is a fantastic resource to research your river walks, based on satellite imagery representing the earth in 3D. You can see landscapes from various angles, zoom in and out, and tilt or rotate the view to look around. This helps you plan your river walks, spot the beaches and find stairs leading down to the river. If Google Earth captures the river landscape when the tide is out you have a birds-eye view for your foreshore plans.

These are popular Thames Beaches:-

- Under the Millennium Bridge on the Thames North Bank.
- Bankside Beach in front of Tate Modern and The Globe Theatre.
- Thames Beach in front of Gabriel's Wharf.
- Bermondsey Beach, Thames South Bank, between Rotherhithe and Tower Bridge.
- Rotherhithe Beach has easy access from Rotherhithe.
- Wapping Beach below King Henry Stairs stretching to The Prospect of Whitby Pub.
- Putney and Fulham beaches.
- Greenwich foreshore in front of The Royal Naval College.

See the Chart listing Thames Beaches.

Thames tourist groups use these areas for access to the foreshore: Wapping Beach, Rotherhithe Beach, Fulham Beach, the beach below the Millennium Bridge, and Greenwich and Deptford Beach.

Extraordinary finds

My favourite mudlarking walks
These are my favourite mudlarking walks, which involve dipping down onto the foreshore. Some are short, like the City of London walk, so you can spend more time searching. Others, like the Putney Bridge walk, can take about 2 hours. Details were correct when we checked the walks, but access to the riverbank is constantly changing, and gates and steps down can be restricted.

You can visit these areas with groups such as Thames Explorer Trust, Thames Discovery Programme, Thames Festival Trust, Southwark Cathedral Walks and the Meetup Group, London Culture Seekers if you don't have a permit, and forage along the shoreline. The group leaders help identify finds. I've been on all of these walks, and the leaders are very knowledgeable. You leave findings on the foreshore (2023 rules).

These are my favourite walks with access to the river.

1. Wapping Walk – North Bank – Tower Bridge to The Prospect of Whitby. Wapping was another busy area of the river. Search in front of the old docks and warehouses, using the narrow alleyways with stairs that lead down to the foreshore.
2. Rotherhithe Walk – South Bank – Tower Bridge to Rotherhithe Beach. Rotherhithe is a historic area of London that was a busy port with shipbuilding and boat repairs, so the wide, sandy beach collects rusty nails, bolts, and metal.
3. Putney Bridge Circular Walk – Putney Bridge to Hammersmith Bridge South Bank returning North Bank
4. South Bank Walk – London Bridge to Royal Festival Hall. Bankside is a favourite area, and there are beaches in front of the Tate Modern and Shakespeare's Globe Theatre in Southwark. The South Bank has wide public beaches where you can mudlark on the foreshore between the OXO Tower and Blackfriars Bridge.

5. City of London Walk – Cannon Street Station to Blackfriars Bridge. On the river's North Bank, beside the Millennium Bridge, there's access down Trig Lane Stairs to the riverbank and onto Queenhithe foreshore.
6. Greenwich – East and West and The Greenwich Foot Tunnel. Greenwich has popular historic sites like the Royal Observatory and the National Maritime Museum and has a wide, sandy foreshore. Access to part of the Greenwich foreshore is prohibited as it's a Scheduled Ancient Monument. Check the Port of London Authority (PLA) map for details.

There's detailed information on each walk at the end.

Rotherhithe Beach

When should you go mudlarking?
You'll be disappointed if you arrive at the river to discover that it's high tide for a few hours. There will be no shoreline to mudlark along, so use a tide table to plan the best time to visit. At the lowest tides, new finds are exposed, things get washed up from the river and visitors drop all sorts of stuff into the water, by mistake or on purpose.

Moon and tides

How does the moon affect the tide? This question puzzled me since I noticed, for the first time, a huge supermoon rising above the river when I was mudlarking opposite The Shard. A great orange ball crept up from the horizon and glowed in the sky. As it climbed higher during the night, the moon's light rippled in the river water. A truly magical sight. Until then, I hadn't connected the moon to the low tides that expert mudlarks enjoy when the river level drops dramatically, revealing hidden treasures.

These days, I put the dates of the full moons and the Neap and Spring Tides on my phone diary so I can plan to mudlark when the river is at its lowest level.

Why do tides happen? The sun and moon exert a gravitational pull on the water, and during a full or new moon, the tidal range is generally higher than during other moon phases. Full or new moon dates are close to low tides when more of the foreshore is exposed. The full moon provides a wonderful natural light to help search during nightlarking, and on a clear night, it's breathtaking to catch the cone of white light that glitters down the river as the moon rises.

It takes the Moon about 29.5 days to go through all of its phases, meaning that each month has, on average, one full moon, so there are 12 in a year, but sometimes we get two full moons in one month. Every couple of weeks, there are Spring Tides when the full tides are exceptionally high and the low tides exceptionally low. Roughly one week after each Spring Tide, there is a Neap Tide when the highs and lows are less extreme. In spring, there are extremely low tides in the daytime, and in summer, there are low tides at night when you need a head torch to search. The best low tides occur every two weeks, linked to the lunar cycles.

If you see a full moon, there will be a Spring Tide a couple of days after. The river flows fastest during Spring Tides and slowest during Neap Tides, so know your escape routes.

Moons of the Year

These names were given to the moons by the North American Indians and are used worldwide, although some have different names in other countries and cultures.

Find out the dates of the moons and put them in your mudlarking diary. Then, if you are a keen mudlark, don't book a holiday on those dates, as you'll be frustrated not to be able to visit the river. A Supermoon is when the full moon is at the point in its orbit closest to Earth, and in the summertime, it glows huge and bright and lights up your river searches if the skies are clear of clouds and the weather is not stormy.

Name of the moon	Why is it given this name?
January: Wolf Moon.	January's full moon is named after the hungry wolves howling due to the lack of food in midwinter.
February: Snow Moon.	When this moon rises, February usually has cold, snowy weather in North America.
March: Worm Moon.	Worm trails appear in newly thawed ground after the winter freeze.
April: Pink Moon	Named the Pink Moon after a species of early blooming wildflower.
May: Flower Moon	May is the month when so many flowers bloom. Other names include the hare moon, the corn planting moon, and the milk moon.

June: Strawberry Moon	In North America, strawberries are harvested in June. In Europe, it's called the rose or the hot moon.
July: Buck Moon	Male deer shed their antlers yearly, and they begin regrowing them in July.
August: Sturgeon Moon	Named by the fishing tribes as the Sturgeon Moon, as it appeared in August when the Great Lakes had plenty of these fish. It's also called the green corn moon, the grain moon, and the red moon as it appears pinky red.
September: Harvest Moon	The moon appears bright and rises early, letting farmers continue harvesting into the night.
October: Hunter's Moon	The Hunter's Moon is startlingly bright, letting hunters stalk their prey at night.
November: Beaver Moon	The name comes from beaver activities in the winter. It's also called the frost moon.
December: Cold Moon	The coming of winter gives December's full moon the name Cold Moon.

Do tides matter?

'Tide and time wait for no man', said Geoffrey Chaucer in the 14th century, and it's wise to remember that when mudlarks are down on our knees searching in the shingle.

It's surprising to find that some London visitors don't know that the river tides go in and out and think there's something wrong with the water levels in the Thames!

Details of tide times are available from the Port of London Authority (PLA) website and the PLA app. The height of the highest and the lowest tides is shown in metres. High tide can be 7 metres, and in certain areas, the river sometimes floods over the pavement and onto the road, so be careful if you park your car nearby. Low tide can be 0.7 metres, a level which is appreciated by mudlarks.

On some parts of the riverbank with wide foreshores, you can mudlark up to 2 hours before and 2 hours after low tide. Rotherhithe Beach has a wide foreshore, but Deptford Beach is narrow, so check maps beforehand. When you visit, watch if the tide is rising or falling. A rising tide is when the river is flowing inland from the sea. A falling tide is when the river is flowing out to the sea. Keep steps, stairs or good-quality riverbank ladders close by to escape. Sometimes, the river water comes in quickly, and you could get trapped at pinch points. When it happened to me, I was quietly terrified as I rushed to the stairs, sinking through the mud in my struggle to get off the foreshore.

Uber Boat

How do I check tide times?
Find the tide times for the River Thames using booklets, websites or apps.

Type 'London Bridge tide times' into Google, and the details come up.

The tide times tables show the predicted high and low tide times and high and low water heights along the Thames. You need to know the low tide times for the areas you visit, such as Putney, Chelsea, or London Bridge. Choose 'Tower' or 'London Bridge' if mudlarking in Central London.

The Port of London Authority's website provides detailed, real-time river level data and tidal predictions for the Thames. This information is updated regularly, and you can download a pdf of their tide times.

Thames Tides show tides for southwest London – Putney Bridge, Chiswick, Strand on the Green, Brentford, and Richmond Lock.

Tide prediction websites	Website
EasyTide	https://easytide.admiralty.co.uk
BBC tide times for London Bridge (Tower Pier)	https://www.bbc.co.uk/weather/coast-and-sea/tide-tables
Willy Weather (Tower Bridge tides)	https://tides.willyweather.co.uk/se/greater-london/river-thames—tower-bridge.html
Port of London Authority's website (PLA)	http://www.pla.co.uk/Safety/Tide-Tables
Thames Tides	http://thamestides.org.uk/todayp
Tide prediction Apps	My Tide Times, Tides Near Me, PLA Tidal Times App, and Magicseaweed.

How to get down to the foreshore

When I travel by Uber Boat up and down the river, I wonder how the mudlarks that I see on the foreshore get down to the riverbank. Some, unlike me, are agile and climb up and down the ladders attached to the river wall, but these ladders can be poorly maintained, don't reach the foreshore or may need you to hike up to get over the river wall. Much of the Thames Path in central London is directly beside the river, and along the way, you find steps, stairs and slipways leading down to the water, making access easy. You can spot mudlarks as you walk along.

In 2002 The City of London recommended that river and foreshore access – the stairs and steps on the Thames – should be opened up where there is a *'historical precedent and a practical need'*. Their report said 'The stairs and steps on the Thames are the surviving links with London's dependence on the river and the central role it played in the City's commerce and everyday life. These should be opened up where there is historical precedent and practical need.' Let's hope visits to the foreshore will encourage repair.

Back to researching access today, Google Maps shows access points if you zoom in for a close look, although they are not often labelled, and stairs and steps may have several different names. Some older stairs are in disrepair, and access may be blocked with locked gates.

If you take an Uber Boat from Putney to Barking or do the reverse journey, Barking to Putney, you'll have fantastic views of the north and south riverbanks, and you can spot the access points along the riverbank from the boat and map them on your phone.

The tour groups list the access points they use, which is a useful starting point.

There's an excellent blog on Wandle News designed by Olivia, who gives useful information on how to get down to the riverbank with clear photos and descriptions of findings.

Stairs

Stairs down to the river may be concrete, wood, or metal, and many get covered in green algae as they are underwater twice a day. They can be steep, uneven, and slippery when wet, so use handrails if available.

In the areas close to the city, watermen used stairs leading down to the river years ago to pick up and drop off passengers crossing the Thames and load and unload cargo. Some of these older stairs are in disrepair and unsafe, and access to the river may be blocked.

Wapping slipway

In 1746 the surveyor and cartographer John Rocque published a map of London listing the stairs on the Thames. One hundred years later Cross's New Plan of London published in 1850 showed more stairs down to the river. Now you can use Google Earth for research.

Type 'River stairs London' into Google Maps and get a list of stairs. These include Horsley Down, King Henry's Stairs, Wapping New Stairs, Alderman Stairs, Trig Lane Stairs, New Crane Stairs, Thames Beach, Pelican Stairs, Rotherhithe Beach all with links to a map for river access and photos.

Slipways
A slipway is a ramp from the shore from which ships or boats can be moved to and from the water. Many slipways were used years ago to launch large ships, and today, they are used for access to launch small boats and canoes in and out of the river.

You may be able to get down some slipways onto the foreshore for mudlarking but check the signage. It is a gentler way to descend onto the riverbank, but you might need permission to use them. You need a licence to paddle a canoe or paddle board on the River Thames. Boats travel on the right-hand side of the river, the opposite of how we drive in the UK.

If you type 'River Slipways London' into Google Maps, you get a list of slipways such as Putney Slipway, Old Swan Wharf Battersea, River Lane Slipway Richmond, and The Dove Pier Slipway.

Here is a list of slipways.

1. Westminster Boating Base has a slipway to the water on the North Bank, near the Houses of Parliament.
2. Whitehall Gardens public park has a slipway on the North Bank, between the Embankment and Westminster Bridge.
3. Victoria Embankment Gardens has a public park slipway between Hungerford Bridge and Waterloo Bridge on the North Bank.
4. Lambeth Pier, on the South Bank near Lambeth Bridge, has a slipway providing river access.
5. Battersea Slipway by St Mary's Church, Battersea Church Rd leads to a shingle beach with lots of litter.

Draw Docks

Draw Docks are the creeks and inlets for unloading barges so they could tie up and wait for the tide to go out. Today, many are used for water activities, and you can sail, canoe, and use larger boats on the river from here. Some have easy access to the foreshore.

Type 'Draw dock Thames London' into Google Maps to get a list of docks, such as Johnson's Draw Dock and Newcastle Draw Dock, which are both on the Isle of Dogs with access to the foreshore.

Thames Beaches

To find a London beach, type 'London beach' into Google Maps, and a list comes up. Click the link to the beach you want to visit and view the uploaded photographs.

If you see a beach at low tide along the foreshore, you have found a place to mudlark. Check access and exit routes as you go down, and take a beach towel to sunbathe on a summer's day.

Beaches appear at low tide and get covered in water at high tide, and some parts of the foreshore are sandy. In 1934, King George V decreed that the beach on Tower Foreshore, by Tower Bridge, could be used by the children of London who should have 'free access forever' and barge-loads of sand were brought in. This artificial beach was a great success. Newspapers wrote that children built sandcastles and swam in the river water while the grownups sat on deckchairs on the sand.

The beach was closed in 1971 due to river pollution, but you'll find sandy beaches along the North and South Banks below the Millenium Bridge and in front of the OXO Tower, where you may see the sand sculptor making interesting creations when the tide goes out. As soon as the tide comes in, the sculpture is washed away, and the next day, he may start again.

Beaches with easy access and sand include Bankside, Thames, Wapping, Rotherhithe and Bermondsey.

See the Beaches Chart at the end for details.

Thames Barrier

Thames Barrier

If you are travelling some distance to visit London to mudlark, check with the Thames Barrier website to see if it's closed that day, as the tide does not flow in and out during this time, and you may not be able to get down to the foreshore. One evening, when I planned to mudlark on a Thames River Festival day, I expected the river to flow out to the sea so I could access the foreshore, but the river water was high for hours. A friendly mudlark told me the Thames Barrier was closed for the festival so there would be no tidal flow, so no mudlarking for me that evening.

The Thames Barrier spans 520 metres across the Thames near Woolwich and protects 125 square kilometres of central London from flooding caused by tidal surges. It has ten steel gates that can be raised into position across the River Thames. When raised, the main gates stand as high as a 5-storey building and as wide as the opening of Tower Bridge.

The barrier is closed under storm surge conditions to protect London from flooding from the sea. It may also be closed during periods of high flow over Teddington Weir, reducing the risk of river flooding in areas of west London, including Richmond and Twickenham. This process takes about 5 hours, and then the barrier is opened, and the upstream water flows out to sea with the outward bound tide.

By April 2023, the Thames Barrier had been closed 208 times since it opened in 1982. The Thames Barrier Information Centre has a small exhibition and you need an appointment to visit.

See the Useful Contacts Website at the end for details.

All about finds

The exposed riverbed in London is the longest archaeological site in Britain, with artefacts from 4,000 years of human activity. The Thames is tidal, and the foreshore is covered with finds from every era – Roman, Medieval, Tudor, Victorian, and today's throwaways.

Over the years, many things have ended up in the River Thames, and the Thames mud is anaerobic, which means it is without oxygen and so a great preservative for lost things in the river. London mudlarks find an amazing range of artefacts on the foreshore – coins, tokens, jettons, buttons, buckles, cufflinks, wig curlers, jewellery, gemstones, red garnets, rings, brooches, clothes fasteners, toys, gaming pieces, dice, dominoes, pilgrim badges, bottles, shoes, pins, daggers, knives, chainmail, pottery and porcelain, early and late stoneware, and of course, clay pipes.

If you want to discover what mudlarks have found, simply type into Google 'Where can you find what things mudlarks find', and a list of links appears.

Another tip is to download copies of old maps, see the past activity on the riverbank in mudlarking areas and find clues about the people living and travelling around the river.

Modern finds on the foreshore

These are some modern things that I frequently find on the foreshore:- NOS capsules, creamers, coloured vapes, jewellery, religious offerings, bikes for hire, shopping trolleys, plastic bottles, plastic and glass beer glasses, credit and hotel plastic cards, clothing, shoes, and bags.

If you fancy litter picking, take an extra carrier bag to collect rubbish from the foreshore and dispose of in rubbish bins. Several voluntary groups collect foreshore rubbish.

Taking things back to the Thames

I frequently take back finds found in the river when I no longer need to keep them, after I have researched and photographed them. A young woman found one of my returned pieces and said, 'This hasn't been touched for 300 years'. I didn't want to spoil her fun by telling her I'd taken it back in the river the previous week.

A famous find of a missing Victoria Cross

In 2015, a metal detectorist named Tobias Neto discovered the lower part of a Victoria Cross (VC) on the banks of the Thames. It was dated 5 November 1854 and awarded for the Battle of Inkerman, an important engagement in the Crimean War 1854-1856. The bar with the name of the recipient attached to the loop was missing, so the owner could not be identified, but only two VCs awarded for Inkerman were unaccounted for. Those were awarded to Privates John McDermond and John Byrne. Inkerman became known as 'the soldiers' battle' as it was small groups of infantry standing firm in the fog who won the day.

The cross was examined using X-ray fluorescence to find its composition, and it was found to be genuine but rather battered after many years in the Thames. How the VC ended up in the Thames is a mystery, and it is still not possible to determine which man it belonged to.

You can find the medal at The National Army Museum.

Victoria Cross

Can I keep what I find?
If you have a licence, you can keep what you find unless the object is treasure or an item of archaeological or historical interest. A treasure is any object found in the UK that is at least 300 years old, contains a minimum amount of gold or silver, or is of significant historical or archaeological interest. Anything qualifying as treasure has to be reported via the Finds Liaison Officer (FLO). Email if you think your find may be of historical interest – see details below.

Can I sell what I find?
Holders of Foreshore Permits may not sell items taken from the foreshore unless special circumstances are agreed with the Port of London Authority (PLA).

What finds must I report?
Report any objects you find that could be of archaeological interest to the Portable Antiquities Scheme Finds Liaison Officer at the Museum of London (swyatt@museumoflondon.org.uk) or on 0207 814 5733.

You can report to any UK FLO.

The Portable Antiquities Scheme (https://finds.org.uk/) records all archaeological finds made by the public in England and Wales. If your finds are treasure, contact the coroner for the district where found, usually within fourteen days of making the find.

In practice, many finders report treasure via the Finds Liaison Officer (FLO), who can also help you identify things you have found. The coroner or FLO will give guidance on what to do. The Treasure Act code of practice contains a directory of coroners in the Thames area.

How can I identify my finds?
If mudlarks are on the riverbank, they may help you identify special finds. So many are generous, incredibly knowledgeable and enjoy sharing. Ask permission first. Check their Instagram and Facebook accounts and ask if you can follow them. You will learn a lot.

Online mudlark groups on Facebook, Instagram, and X offer great advice. If you get permission to join, post your photographs and ask for help. When I thought a piece of knapped flint was a sharp tool, they told me kindly, no, it was just a piece of sandstone, bashed about by the river, which humans had not worked on, and I should keep searching.

My tip on storing special finds – some older items like beads and coins are very tiny. Take a small pot to put small finds in. I once used a plastic bag and lost things through a hole in the bottom.

How do I clean my finds?

I always wash my finds in soapy water and rub them dry with a cloth, but when I found a pewter medallion, I left it in vinegar in the hope that the acid would effervesce off some of the lumps. Then I gave it a rub with a Scotchbrite pad, took a photograph, asked an expert what it was, and admitted my cleaning techniques. There was shock at my destructive cleaning. The advice was to use soap and water, clean it with a soft toothbrush, and then leave it. Surface soil can be removed with cotton buds and water and eased with a cocktail stick. But no scrubbing. Distilled water is best, as tap water contains chlorine.

If you think your find is precious, don't do any cleaning and get advice from experts such as the Portable Antiquities Scheme (PAL).

The following notes are PAL's advice on How to Clean Finds. If things have been in the river mud for hundreds of years, they may not last long when exposed to air as they begin to decay and corrode.

Here are their tips.

- Gold does not corrode, but if it's not pure, it may look brown, green or orange and should be kept separate in a storage box.
- Silver can be shiny, but it may be black and corroded with lumps and can crack.
- Iron becomes a brown lump as it corrodes, so keep it dry.
- Pewter is a tin-based alloy that looks like lead, but the surface can be brittle, so don't scrub.
- Leather looks almost black when it comes out of the wet mud, and as it dries out, it crumbles and shrinks, so get advice if you think you've found something special, like pieces of a Tudor shoe.
- The colour of glass bottles and shards in the river can change over time as the colourants decay. If you think it's treasure, report it to FLO.

- Lead is a dark grey colour and feels heavy. If you find a small reel of lead, unfold it as there may be a surprise inside – it could unravel and become a spoon.

Here are some further tips:
Lemon juice and vinegar are harsh chemicals and can damage surfaces.

Store things in a plastic box with silica gel packs to absorb water.

Coins should not be straightened as they may be brittle and crack.

If you're storing finds in a plastic bag, make holes to prevent condensation.

Label your finds so that you remember all the research like where and when you found them and what you think they are.

The Society of Thames Mudlarks

The Society of Thames Mudlarks was founded in the late 1970s, and the members were granted a special mudlarking licence from the Port of London Authority. It's a select group restricted to around 50 members. Thanks to the Society, tens of thousands of historically important artefacts were acquired by the Museum of London, which has one of the largest collections in the world of Medieval pilgrim badges and Post-Medieval pewter toys. Members work closely with the Museum of London Archaeology (MOLA).

In 2009, one of the founder members of the society, Tony Pilson, donated a collection of over two and a half thousand buttons dating from the 14th to the late 19th century, which he found along the Thames foreshore. Members are the only people with an exclusive Digging Permit, which allows, on certain parts of the North shore, excavation to a maximum depth of 1.3 metres. Some members use metal detectors to search for metal valuables.

The British Museum

Pilgrim Badge

The British Museum database has 1.4 million items in its Collection, quite a few provided by mudlarks. To search on the British Museum website for things found in the Thames, type in 'Collection, Search, Keyword, Thames, River' and discover over 2000 finds listed from the Thames with photographs to help you identify things. Look up an item such as a pilgrim badge and find where it was discovered.

These are some of the categories: – adze, ampullae, amulet rings, animal remains, arrowheads, awls and axes – flint axes from Neolithic and Bronze Age, beads, belt fittings, bracelets, brooches, buckles, chains, and cloth seals.

The database describes the object, may show a photograph and identifies where it was discovered. So a Neolithic, Bronze Age flaked flint axe with a polished blade was found beside the Thames in Hammersmith, which shows that people were around that part of the river thousands of years ago.

A Medieval pilgrim ampulla (1275 – 1375) made of lead alloy, associated with the shrine of Thomas Becket Canterbury, was found beside the Thames, City of London, Cannon Street, which was near the site of the old London Bridge.

As you search their database, you'll learn a lot and many have detailed descriptions and photographs, so a useful, free research tool for mudlarks.

London Bridge

London Bridge crosses the central area of the river, which is a favourite place to mudlark. Until the mid-eighteenth century, the Old London Bridge was the only crossing on the Thames, and this may be why mudlarks find so many things have fallen in the river, as people would cross over on boats if the bridge became too crowded. There is an information board on the new steps from London Bridge to the Thames Path, which tells the story of the Bridge, shows the aquatic diversity of the wildlife on the river and shows the famous nursery rhyme. You may remember it from childhood and be able to sing along or know the game where two children form an arch for the other children to pass through.

The rhyme starts like this, and there are many verses: –

London Bridge is falling down
Falling down, falling down
London Bridge is falling down
My fair Lady
Build it up with iron bars
Iron bars, iron bars
Build it up with iron bars
My fair Lady

The rhyme dates back to the 17th century, but historians are not certain of its meaning. It may be because the bridge needed constant building and repair work before it was replaced. The old London Bridge had nineteen narrow arches, which restricted river traffic and water flow, and houses with shops were constructed all the way across. A new London Bridge was opened in 1831 and survived until it was replaced in 1972 when the 1831 bridge was dismantled and reconstructed in Lake Havasu City, Arizona, United States. There is a popular rumour that the bridge was bought in the mistaken belief that it was London's more recognizable Tower Bridge but this was denied by the buyers.

You can see a model of the Old London Bridge in the lovely church of St Magnus of the Martyr on Lower Thames Street. The model was built in 1987 by David T. Aggett and shows the overhanging buildings, a chapel and all the arches of the bridge as it spanned the river from north to south bank. If you go outside the church into the churchyard, you are standing in a place that was once a bustling area where people made their way to and fro from the old London Bridge from 1176 to 1831.

Southwark Bridge

The Thames Ecology

What about pollution?

During the summer of 1858, the River Thames in central London gave off such a foul stench that newspapers called it The Great Stink. The smell from untreated human waste and industrial effluent was so bad that Parliament was closed, and hundreds of tons of lime were tossed into the water to get rid of the smell.

An article in The Illustrated London News commented that:

'We can colonise the remotest ends of the earth; we can conquer India; .... but we cannot clean the River Thames.'

The scientist, Michael Faraday, wrote at the time that 'Near the bridges the feculence rolled up in clouds so dense that they were visible at the surface, ... the whole river was for the time a real sewer.'

Sir Joseph Bazalgette, a civil engineer, was employed in the 1850s to create a sewage system for central London, which cleaned up the river and helped relieve the City from cholera epidemics which had killed so many. London still relies on this 150-year-old sewer system built for a population less than half its current size. As a result, millions of tonnes of raw sewage spill untreated into the River Thames each year and still enters the Thames when the system reaches capacity at overflow points along the river, such as at Blackfriars. Be careful if you are mudlarking nearby, especially if you think you get whiffs of a bad smell. Remember to wear protective gloves when handling things on the foreshore.

In 1957, the Thames was declared biologically dead by the Natural History Museum as nothing could survive in the water, so in the 1960s, London's sewage system needed to be improved again.

In 2015, the construction of the Thames Tideway Tunnel began, building a 25 km Super Sewer under the Thames to intercept spillages and sewage and clean up the river. The Tunnel is due to be completed in 2025 costing £3.9bn and will capture most of the sewage that enters the river from sewer systems.

London's population is estimated to increase to 16 million by 2160, and the Tideway Tunnel should protect the river from sewage spillage for at least the next 100 years.

Extra note – Bazalgette was incredibly busy around the Thames not only creating a sewage system but also designing Putney and Hammersmith Bridges, which you can visit on the Putney to Hammersmith walk.

Personal note

Recently, I went down to the riverbank to mudlark, just after a fierce rainstorm. Sometimes, when it's rained, the river churns up new things as it swirls up and down with the tides. As I searched along the shingle, I was puzzled to find piles of used tampons, sanitary towels, wet wipes and toilet paper. From the smell, it soon became clear that I was not mudlarking but walking through oodles of soft poo, so I abandoned my lark and swiftly left, not picking anything up.

What had happened? It seems a storm drain had filled up with surface water and sewage, which had then gushed down an outlet into the Thames. Speaking to the people working on the new Super Sewer, Tideway, it seems that this can happen after storms, and I had been lucky not to see it before when I'd been searching the foreshore. I reported the incident to Thames Water, who quickly investigated. The Tideway team is fixing the storm drain, but the problem won't be solved for over a year. In the meantime, I'll avoid the area and always wear gloves when I'm picking things up from the river. Poor geese, ducks and herons. How will the clams, crabs, eels and tiny fish survive if such filth is dumped so frequently into their watery environment?

Plastic waste

Plastic waste and microplastics are major pollutants in the Thames. Between 2016 and 2020, 17,770 single-use plastic bottles, almost half of which were plastic water bottles, were counted and removed at sites along the tidal Thames. Thames21 and the Port of London Authority (PLA) remove over 200 tonnes of waste each year, much of it plastic.

The most frequently found plastic items recovered from the river in the last five years by teams from The River Café were cotton bud sticks, bottle lids, takeaway containers, polystyrene cups, and Wet Wipes. In summer 2022, a Wet Wipe Island, the size of two tennis courts, was found in Hammersmith, changing the course of the river.

Sometimes, the river water looks murky as it carries a huge amount of muddy sediment from its inland source to the North Sea. In lockdown, when only a few boats went up and down the river, the foreshore and the river became muddier. Once the Uber Boats, the pleasure boats, and other river traffic returned, the water was churned up, and the waves and swell washed and changed the muddy foreshore, exposing more of the sediment for mudlarks to search.

The Seine and 2024 Olympics

For 100 years, swimming was banned in the River Seine because the levels of water pollution could make people ill. In the past 20 years, the drainage system for the river has been improved by building an underground reservoir to store the excess water during heavy rain. After more than 1.4 billion euros (£1.2bn) of investment, in July 2023, the French government said that the Seine, in the centre of Paris, would soon be ready to welcome back swimmers and play host to three Olympic events in 2024 – the triathlon, marathon swimming and paratriathlon.

Wildlife and Ecology

The River Thames is full of aquatic wildlife. At least 115 species of fish, 350 species of invertebrates and 92 species of birds use the river. Shrimps, mud snails and eels live in the water, birds use the river for their migratory routes and feeding grounds, and the algae and seaweed that grow on the foreshore provide a place for fish to spawn and feed.

Wild swimming

Improvement in river quality is great news for a river that was declared biologically dead in 1957. However, in 2021, scientists warned that the tidal Thames was suffering from rising nitrate levels as a result of industrial runoff and sewage discharges and that water levels and temperatures were rising due to global warming. So, the work continues.

In 2021, The Zoological Society of London said that the Thames water quality has 'exhibited some promising improvements', with reduced phosphorus concentrations.

See the Wildlife Chart of the River Thames at the end for more information.

Swans

All along the Thames, you will see large, white swans, sometimes with a brood of grey feathered cygnets. They may come up to you expecting to be fed, but give them something more nutritious than bread to eat such as wheat grain, seeds, and vegetables like chopped cabbage and frozen peas. I sometimes pick up the white swan feathers from the foreshore. White feathers are thought to be a signal that someone who has passed away is reaching out to contact you, so they bring back special memories.

The aristocracy ate swans until Tudor times when mute swans were declared the property of the monarch, and killing one was a treasonable offence. After that time, swans stopped being a popular dish. The Swan Act passed in 1788 said, 'No Swan in this land shall be passed through any citizen's mouth (or other entry to the body). If found doing so you shall be sentenced to death by pecking.' That's a strange fact and there's no evidence of that punishment.

Swan Upping is a 900-year-old ceremony which takes place on the Thames every July, and Swan Uppers make a head count of all the mute swans on the river and check them for any signs of injury, commonly caused by fishing hooks and lines. Today, it is more of a census and welfare check for the birds, which are weighed and ringed. A flotilla of traditional Thames rowing skiffs, manned by

Swan Uppers, row their way steadily up the Thames. They are a fabulous sight, dressed in scarlet rowing shirts and headed by The King's Swan Marker, who wears a hat topped with a white swan's feather. When a family of swans and cygnets is spotted, the Swan Uppers carefully position their boats around the swans, lift them from the water and check their health.

You will find a flock of swans gathering on Ratcliff Beach,12 Narrow St, E14 8DH which are fed each day by local residents. Stand and watch as they glide by and get an Instagrammable photo of them on the river in front of the skyscrapers of Canary Wharf.

Wild swimming in the Thames
The tidal Thames is a fast-flowing waterway and the busiest inland waterway in the UK, with over 20,000 ship movements and hosting over 400 special events each year. The River Thames east of Teddington is not suitable for swimming as the water is too polluted and too busy with boats travelling up and down, so if you want to swim, visit places inland on the Thames, away from London, in Berkshire and Oxfordshire.

Check the water quality before setting off – The Rivers Trust provides information on sewage and storm discharge into rivers.

Eel

What to wear to swim

Wild swimming organisations suggest you swim with a fully inflatable raft that comes with a rucksack to carry drying robes, walking boots, and layers of clothes needed for a day in and out of the water. Swim in wet suits as the water can be cold and protect your feet with swimming shoes. Employ a guide if you don't know the river access points and safety issues. Make sure you can be seen in the water – wear a brightly coloured swim hat and coloured float.

Food and drink finds

As I wander along the foreshore, I find things that tell me so much about the history of the food and drink consumed by Londoners over the years. Each object begs some research. Why are there so many oyster shells on the river bank? Are eels still found in the river? What is the story around these shards of old gin and beer bottles on the shoreline? What curious foods were traded and eaten in this busy city?

Here are just a few food and drink puzzles that I've unravelled from my river finds.

Oysters

If you mudlark anywhere along the Thames foreshore, you will crunch over oyster shells, some with round or square holes and some looking old and battered.

Most of the old, flat shells belong to the native British oysters, an important food source for Londoners for centuries. The Romans cultivated oyster beds in the river, but as the river became more polluted as the population of London increased, for safety, oysters were grown further out towards the sea in oyster beds along the Thames Estuary in Kent and Essex, then shipped to Billingsgate Market. For many years, oysters provided an inexpensive food for London people from all walks of life.

Samuel Pepys is famous for his diaries, which provide a fascinating glimpse of London life in the 1660s. He wrote a lot about eating oysters and described how, in 1665, he visited his London oyster shop on Gracious Street, bought two barrels of oysters sourced from Colchester and enjoyed them for dinner with friends. A barrel then would have been the size of a very large can. Were his oysters still in their shells or shucked? Not many oysters with their shells would fit in a can but maybe Samuel had his own oyster knife to prize open the shells.

Rock Oyster

Charles Dickens wrote in 1836, 'Poverty and oysters always seem to go together,' so oysters in those days were eaten by everyone.

In the past 200 years, the oyster population in the Thames has declined, but there are still oyster fisheries in Essex and Kent. Native oysters are flatter than other varieties, their meat content is much smaller, but they are appreciated for their taste. Whitstable in Kent has an annual Oyster Festival, where you can try different types of oysters, like rock oysters, and visit their oyster beds with an oyster farmer. Walk along the beach in front of the restaurants and see piles of oyster shells, which the sea, in time, will break down into sand, just like the oysters on the Thames riverbed. Read my story of the London Oyster Card and decide if it's linked to the holey oyster shells on the riverbank.

Sugar

When I picked up a chunk of reddish-brown unglazed pottery from the foreshore, with thin streaks of white slip on one side, I had no idea what it was or how this story would unravel. When I showed it to an expert mudlark he said,

'It's a piece from a sugar cone. There's loads on the riverbank.' Then he hurried off for a cup of tea, maybe stirring in a few spoonfuls of sugar.

Sugar was available in Britain from the 12th century, but it was gritty and used as a spice or medicine. The process of refining sugar existed in the Middle East long before it was introduced to Europe in the 1400s.

There's a Flemish print called Saccharum from the 16th century in the British Museum, which explains the process of sugar refining. It's part of a series of prints on new inventions and discoveries of that time from Sir Hans Sloane's collection. The process starts with chopping sugar cane into chunks, extracting, then boiling the juice, and pouring the liquid into the cones. When set, the sugar loaves are eased out of the moulds, taking care not to damage them. Cones came in different sizes, some a few inches tall, others a foot in height and the small cones were used to make the expensive white sugar.

Elizabeth I, who reigned England from 1558 to 1603, was particularly fond of sugar, and she used a Tudor toothpaste, made from sugar, for brushing her teeth, so by her fifties, most of her teeth were rotten, had fallen out or turned black.

From Medieval times and up until the 19th century, sugar was sold in solid form, and sugar loaves took pride of place on the dining tables of smart houses during the 18th century. Sugar nippers were used to cut off small bits of sugar from the sugar cone for guests to taste.

So what's my piece of sugar cone doing on the riverbank? The sugar cane was brought in ships for processing in small factories along the river, and broken sugar cone moulds were probably thrown away after use into the water. Sugar cane was grown in plantations in America and the Caribbean, and British companies thrived on the profits of enslaved labour. Why does my piece have lines of white slip? The slip stops the sugar from sticking to the inside of the mould, and the finished intact sugar loaf would have been precious.

If you want to try a modern version of the sugar loaf, buy a chunk of jaggery, available in Asian food shops. It's made from the juice of crushed sugar cane, which is boiled and concentrated to a golden brown colour and then cooled and poured into pans to set. Cut small chunks off the jaggery block, just like people did with the sugar loaf years ago, and enjoy the rich taste of molasses. It's used to sweeten food and drinks, and some people believe it has medicinal properties. But remember, it is sugar.

The Story of Tate and Lyle Sugar

Henry Tate and Sons opened the Thames Refinery for sugar in 1878 at Silvertown, near The Thames in East London, and in 1882, Abram Lyle opened Lyle's Golden Syrup factory nearby. In 1921, they merged to become the famous company Tate & Lyle and their Thames Refinery, was once the largest sugar refinery in the world, processing around 50% of the world's sugar.

Why is Henry Tate famous? He made his fortune as a sugar refiner and spent money collecting British nineteenth-century art. In 1889, he offered his art collection to the nation and provided funding for the first Tate Gallery, which is now called Tate Britain. Today, there are four Tate Galleries in the UK, and the story all goes back to sugar.

Eels

As you mudlark along the riverbank, you may, sadly, find the body of a tiny eel lying on the shore. Eels were one of the few types of freshwater fish that could survive as the Thames became more polluted, but now there are few in the river, and they should not be eaten. Why do they live in the Thames? Eels begin their lives in the Sargasso Sea, cross the Atlantic Ocean, navigate up freshwater rivers, like the Thames, to feed and grow, and then return to the Sargasso Sea to breed just once in their lifetime.

Billingsgate Fish Market started on the banks of the Thames in the 16th century, and eels were brought there for sale from Europe along with those caught in the river.

Jellied eels became a popular, cheap food for London's working class in the 18th century, and piemen walked the city streets carrying trays piled with eel-filled pies on their heads. Fish shops sold live or cooked eels, and in the City, you could eat jellied eels from stalls outside the pubs. By the 19th century many high streets in east and southeast London had Pie 'n' Mash shops serving minced beef pie with a side dish of jellied eels, and some of their marble floors were scattered with sawdust to collect the eel bones that customers spat out.

Manze's Pie and Eel shop

Today if you want to eat eels, visit M. Manze's Pie 'n' Mash shop at 87 Tower Bridge Road, although there was no sawdust on the floor on my trip. It was bought by Michele Manze in 1902 and is the oldest pie and eel shop still in business in 2023. Choose a dish of jellied eels or hot stewed eels, followed by a meat pie, mash and green liquor. This green gravy used to be made from eel juice, but now it's a thin parsley sauce. These days, Manze's get their eels from Northern Ireland as there's no supply from the Thames. The Thames Barrier may have stopped the young elvers from travelling upriver.

Whales

If you're mudlarking in Rotherhithe, you can see a whalebone as part of the structure of the barge bed in front of Brandram's Wharf at Rotherhithe Beach, but it is eroding quickly with the swell of the tides. The bone was discovered in 2012 by a group from the Thames Discovery Programme, which did a foreshore survey, and they also found a large whale vertebra nearby.

During the 18th century, London was a leading whaling port, and thousands of whales and seals were killed in the cold waters around Greenland, and their bodies were brought back to Greenland Dock in Southwark for processing.

The whale blubber was rendered down in the boiling houses of Rotherhithe, where the stink and smell of rotting flesh must have been awful. The resulting oil was used for soap, paint, and domestic and street lighting. Corsets and hooped petticoats, called farthingales, worn by fashionable ladies of the time, were made from whalebones, larger bones became gate posts and arches or were used for ship repair, with left-over bits made into fertiliser.

Did the British ever eat whale meat? Yes, in the Second World War, when food was in short supply. Huge factory ships were built for the whalers as whale oil and flesh became increasingly important to supplement wartime fat and meat rations. The government promoted whale meat as an unrationed alternative to beef, claiming that it tasted the same and had similar health benefits. Corned whale meat, called 'Whacon', was introduced in 1951 as an alternative to corned beef, although it was never a popular dish. Commercial whaling was finally banned by the International Whaling Commission (IWC) during the seasons 1986–90, but some countries continue to hunt them.

Have a drink in the Ship and Whale Pub next to Greenland Dock, one of the oldest original buildings in the area, as a reminder of our whaling history.

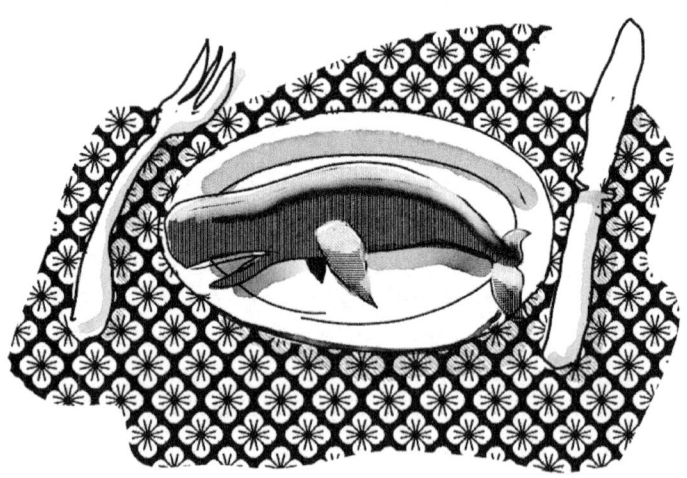

Whale meat

Burgess's Anchovy Paste
Most mudlarks love picking up things from the river with names on them. It gives us the start to research and a chance to connect with others. The crazed, stained half piece of a white ceramic lid poking out of the river mud led me on a deep dive into Victorian

food habits. The smart black letters had been transferred onto the glaze and read BURGESS'S Genuine The Original 107 The Strand corner of. At the top of the lid, there's a crest with a crown, maybe a lion's head and a unicorn and the words SOIT QUI MAL. I'm told it's mid-19th century, black transferware with a Royal Warrant and Queen Victoria's crown.

A quick search on eBay led to finding an intact lid for sale. This one read Burgess's Genuine Anchovy Paste for Toast Biscuit & C The Original Sauce Warehouse 107 Strand Corner of the Savoy Steps London. Letters around the crest read HONI SOIT QUI MAL Y PENSE and DIEU ET MON DROIT, and the eBay seller says it's from the 1890s.

So what's its story? John Burgess had a London business importing Italian hams and olive oil, and he was first mentioned in the rate book for the Strand in 1774. 107 Strand is near the Strand Palace Hotel, so if he'd stayed there it would now be a very smart place to run a business. Burgess introduced his Essence of Anchovies in 1775, made from anchovies, water, and spices and it was the first branded sauce to become widely known around the country. His only son, William, joined his father in 1800, and the company was known as John Burgess & Son. By 1805, their products were on board Admiral Nelson's HMS Victory at the Battle of the Nile and Trafalgar, Lord Byron wrote of Burgess's fish sauce in his poem Beppo, and the novelist Walter Scott claimed that Burgess made the best fish sauce. So, the company got involved with some great promotions.

In 1908, the factory moved to Willesden, and the company were appointed purveyors to George V in 1911. That same year, Captain Scott took several bottles of Burgess's Essence of Anchovies with him to the Antarctic, as it had a long shelf life, and its strong fishy flavour would have perked up the ship's biscuits.

Competition arrived with similar products, and sales steadily declined. The brand name was taken over several times and is no longer sold in supermarkets.

Burgess's Anchovy Paste

If you want to make anchovy paste, these are the ingredients: – salted anchovies, butter, breadcrumbs, cayenne pepper, ground cinnamon, ground nutmeg, and ground black pepper. Use a mortar and pestle or a food processor to pound the anchovies and butter to a smooth paste. Stir in the breadcrumbs, spices and pepper and spoon the paste into a large ramekin. Cover and chill before serving with toast, as they suggest on my pot lid. People who tasted my recipe say it's delicious, and you can dollop it on baked potatoes or stir it into sauces to add an intense flavour.

Today, you can buy a ready-made anchovy paste called Patum Peperium, The Gentleman's Relish, a spiced anchovy relish created in 1828 by an Englishman, John Osborn. You'll be eating a piece of history which, to keep it affordable, is now sold in a plastic pot.

London Dry Gin

An emerald-green square glass base from a bottle found on the riverbank led me on another journey, this time into spirits. My piece matched finds of green glass shards embossed with letters from Gordon's Special Dry London Gin and Established 1769, which mudlarks helped me identify. So what's the story? Who was Gordon? Why is it called Dry London Gin? And why are there so many pieces from gin bottles in the river?

Let's start with Alexander Gordon. My piece of glass has a strange shape stamped on the base, which turns out to be the Gordon's Gin company's trademark of a wild boar, created from the legend that a member of the Gordon clan saved the King of Scotland from a wild boar when out hunting. The boar became their trademark and is still used on their bottles today.

Back in the 17th century, London was suffering from what was called The Gin Craze – a bit like today where so many types of gin are for sale in supermarkets. William of Orange had ascended the British throne in 1688, France became the enemy, and the government restricted imports of French brandy. Up until then, people had been drinking Holland's Gin, known also as Genever, brought back by soldiers during the Thirty Years War in the 17th century. Basically, the name gin comes from the French word genièvre, which is the French word for genever, and genever is the Dutch word for juniper. Double Dutch, perhaps.

From the 1730s, gin began being made in small gin distilleries around London, with over 7,000 gin shops selling a cheap, strong alcoholic drink of variable quality. In poorer areas of London, gin consumption increased, gin joints allowed women to drink alongside men for the first time, and gin became known as Mother's Ruin as drunken parents neglected their children. William Hogarth's famous 1751 print, *Gin Lane,* shows an inner London slum ravaged by drunkenness. The historian of the time, Thomas Fielding, wrote,

'A new kind of drunkenness, unknown to our ancestors, is lately sprung up among us. The drunkenness I here intend is ... by this poison called Gin.'

The Gin Act of 1751, aimed at stopping the overindulgence by poorer people, reduced the number of gin shops and encouraged 'respectable' gin, with a better quality London Dry Gin made in legal distilleries. The term 'Dry' describes spirits distilled with juniper and other botanicals, and 'London' was because this type of gin was made in the capital. So this is where Alexander Gordon stepped in. He was a Londoner of Scot's descent who opened his first gin distillery in 1769 in Southwark, a district known for its reliable water supply. Gordon insisted on top quality distillation of his alcohol and flavoured his Special London Dry Gin with plenty of juniper, the recipe for which remains unchanged to this day. He was also clever at promotion, and his gin became the unofficial drink of the British Navy, which acted as its global ambassador. Today, the company advertises that Gordon's is the world's best-selling gin.

In recent years, sales of gin have soared, and small distilleries have opened in London, which are winning prizes for their taste and flavour. Hopefully, future mudlarks won't find their empty bottles on the Thames foreshore. I haven't answered my question about why there are so many shards of gin bottles in the river, but perhaps they were taken on summer picnics, poured into glasses for gin and tonic and the empties thrown in the water.

Gordon's Gin Boars Head

Batey's Ginger Beer

On my mudlarking patch of the riverbank, I've picked up several thick green glass shards embossed with bits of the letters of BATEY and LONDON, but I've never found a complete bottle. Perhaps my area has been too well scoured by better mudlarks. One piece of glass that makes me smile has large letters saying '¼ d deposit charged on this bottle', but clearly, the owner did not care to return it for a farthing – the name of ¼ d – and tossed it into the river instead. Online research shows that my bottles might have been embossed with BATEY & CO LTD, LONDON, a company that, in late Victorian and early Edwardian times, was famous for making ginger beer.

So what's their story? William Batey started his ginger beer factory on Kingsland Road, south of the Regents Canal, around 1853. He became bankrupt in 1881, and the business was bought by Richard James Alabaster, who established Batey as a limited company in 1887. Alabaster died in 1937, and Batey & Co. continued as an independent company until it was sold to Charrington & Co. Ltd in 1952.

Robert White was another entrepreneur who started selling home-brewed ginger beer from a wheelbarrow in London in 1845. He diversified into making lemonade, and his family's name is still on the label of White's Lemonade, sold in supermarkets. Mudlarks find plenty of White's old lemonade bottles, along with their vulcanite screwtop stoppers labelled R. White, in the river today.

Commercial ginger beer became popular in Britain and its colonies in the 18th century, linked to the increase in trade of sugarcane and ginger root from the Caribbean and Asia. Ginger beer was brewed using yeast, ginger, sugar, and water, and cream of tartar or lemon juice was sometimes added to the recipe. The finished drink was up to 11% alcohol by volume, so at that time, ginger beer was the strength of some wines.

In 1855, the British Parliament passed an Act that imposed an excise tax on beverages with an alcohol content above 2%, so most ginger beer brewers reduced the alcohol content in their products to 2% by using a shorter fermentation time and adding water, which kept the drink affordable and low in alcohol.

After it was brewed, ginger beer was often corked inside stoneware bottles. Part of the reason for packaging in stoneware rather than glass bottles was to hide the grey, cloudy appearance of the ginger beer. What made Batey's use their green glass bottles instead of stoneware? Well, one reason might be that their glass was really thick, so you couldn't see the colour of the drink inside. In 1913, Batey Co. Ltd was taken to court by a Mr Bates, who was clearly displeased with the way his ginger beer was bottled. The outcome of that case went like this:

'Regarding In Bates v. Batey Co. Ltd, the defendants, ginger-beer manufacturers, were held not liable to a consumer for injury occasioned by the bottle bursting as the result of a defect of which the defendants did not know, but which by the exercise of reasonable care they could have discovered.'

History does not explain what injury Mr Bates suffered from.

Most of the ginger beers on sale today are non-alcoholic and made from carbonated sweetened water flavoured with ginger. Shops sell Crabbie's Original Alcoholic Ginger Beer, and their advertising says it's 'The Original Alcoholic Ginger Beer' since 1801, and it looks like John Crabbie beat both Batey and White to the award for producing the first commercial ginger beer.

Sacred and Mindful

Sacred Things in the Thames

In 1970, the Thames was blessed as a sacred river but it has been used for votive offerings for thousands of years.

In the British Museum, you can see the Battersea Shield (350–50 BCE) and the Wandsworth Shield (2nd century BCE), both believed to be votive offerings to the Gods, and both found in the Thames in the 19th century. The Battersea Shield is a sheet of decorated bronze covering a wooden shield and is one of the most significant pieces of Celtic Art found in Britain.

In the Middle Ages, pilgrims returning from important pilgrimages occasionally placed their religious badges in the river for good fortune. Did they imagine that mudlarks would find their precious souvenirs on the River Thames foreshore hundreds of years later? Southwark Cathedral sometimes has a guest exhibition of Medieval pilgrim badges, many of which were found in the Thames close to the Cathedral. The company, Lionheart Replicas, makes very fine, accurate copies of the surviving pewter badges, which you can buy online.

See Useful Contacts.

Today, many people make offerings to the Thames, and I once found a carton containing someone's ashes – the label gave their name and cremation date – which I left in the river. Diwali is a special time for London's large community of Hindus, and the river is used for religious rites, just like the Ganges in India. Mudlarks have found ornately patterned brass plates known as Sri Yantra, which act to ward off evil spirits, decorated coconuts which contain messages to bring good fortune, voodoo dolls spiked with nails and silk bundles bound with a red thread containing offerings of seeds and sweet corn and sometimes coins.

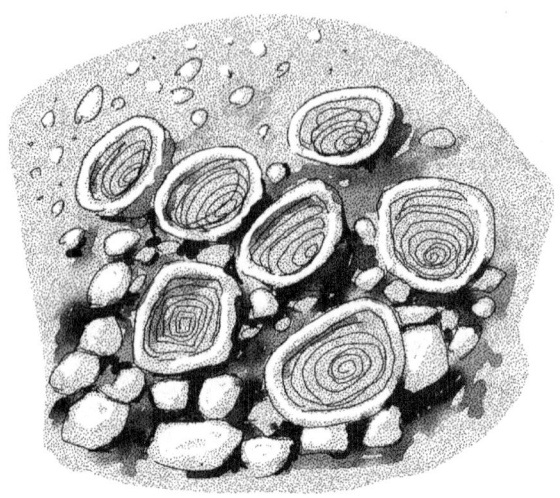

Diwali Pots

What have I found?
In a special part of the river, I find brightly coloured plastic bangles tossed from the overhead bridge, which I assume are sent out for good luck.

After the Diwali celebrations for the Festival of Lights, tiny red clay pots get scattered on the foreshore, and these pots, called diyas, were probably floated down the Thames as part of the ceremony, filled with oil or ghee, inserted with a wick and lit. These little lights are put around the home and in businesses in Hindu homes across India and around the world to celebrate Diwali. Lighting the diya is an act of worship, and it pays homage to Lakshmi, the goddess of prosperity and wealth. Worshippers reflect on their blessings and give thanks.

Ganesh

After one Diwali, I found two statues of Ganesh and Lakshmi, one battered but still colourful, the other plastic and sprayed gold. Should I pick up offerings from the river? Several mudlarks felt that their power had passed to the people who threw them into the river, so it was OK, and a Hindu friend said I would be blessed as I rescued the deities Ganesh and Laksmi from the mud. She said Ganesh is the Hindu god of new beginnings, success, wisdom, and the removal of obstacles, so I need to care for them. So yes, I took them home. But I'm still puzzled whether it's the right thing to do. One mudlark told a journalist he always takes coconuts home from the foreshore as they may be filled with personal items and also money, but on an online forum, people challenged removing offerings from the river. However, the Battersea and Wandsworth Shields were both votive offerings rescued from the river and are now on display in the British Museum. My plastic bangles and statues will, in time, break down and pollute the water. So, should sacred things be picked up or not?

Is mudlarking mindful?

If you read some answers to my question 'Why do you mudlark?' it's clear that searching the foreshore gives mudlarks peace and tranquillity and calms their busy lives. One definition for mindfulness says, 'Mindfulness is the practice of being in the present and fully engaged in the current moment, without judgement or distraction.'

For me, this is true when I'm mudlarking.

So, is mudlarking mindful? I certainly feel calmer and less stressed after I've spent a few hours on the foreshore. It's become a habit, like some people need to go jogging, and I feel the urge to escape to the riverbank as often as possible.

Other mudlarks often say they love the peace and solitude of their time on the riverbank. It's a time to slow down, away from the busy world, to be thoughtful, and find a place for reflection – all keywords and phrases linked to mindfulness.

When you mudlark, you focus on the present moment, with attention to detail, looking for items hidden beneath the sand, shingle and mud, concentrating on the now and the task at hand. It's a thoughtful time in a surprisingly quiet and serene environment which encourages introspection, allowing a moment to process thoughts and emotions.

On the riverbank in all weathers, you connect with nature as you are outside, beside flowing water, noticing clouds passing overhead, with birds and boats to keep you company. Sit and spend time just listening to the surrounding sounds – the flow of water, the whoosh of the river traffic, the squawk of seagulls and the chatter of people. Notice how time has passed and how the challenges of the day seem to settle. Mudlarking is a time to stop, focus, and think and there's that extra connection to history and the past. There's evidence too that mindfulness can lower blood pressure, improve sleep and even help people cope with pain, so yes, I reckon mudlarking is a mindful activity, and it certainly improves my well-being.

Does mudlarking make people happy?
These are some replies from Mudlarks to this question.

'It's fun. It's the thrill of the hunt, the excitement and reward of finding interesting or unique artefacts and that makes me happy.'

'Finding a rare or historically significant item is exhilarating, especially if you can share it with others at meetings and on the online mudlark groups.'

'You focus on searching and being present in the moment – it clears your mind and reduces stress.'

'It connects to the history and culture of a place, to the people who lived and worked there centuries ago, and gives an insight into how these people lived their daily lives – that's exciting to discover. And I'm so happy when I mudlark.'

'It's a very social activity, meeting like-minded people and sharing finds. Some people like to mudlark quietly on their own and enjoy the solitude, but sometimes, there is joy in sharing a special find.'

'Many mudlarks are really happy to share surprising things from their collecting bags and treasure tins and teach the rest of us so much about the history of the river.'

'We make friendships and I learn from them, admire them, develop my own skills and feel a sense of belonging to a place, culture and the world. And we laugh. A lot.'

The combination of the thrill of the hunt, the mindfulness and relaxation, the connection to history, and the social side all contribute to making mudlarking a happy and rewarding experience for many people, including me.

What will mudlarks find in 500 years?
Will there be enough treasure left in the river in hundreds of years? This question was answered by a panel of experts at a Mudlark meeting.

They reckon there'll be plenty of plastic stuff, mobile phones, coins, plastic spectacles, credit cards, vapes, and messages in plastic bottles. Sadly, the Wet Wipe Mountain may be larger and include disposable products we don't know about yet.

The Thames foreshore is constantly eroding, and in 500 years, the river will still wash up treasures for mudlarks to find.

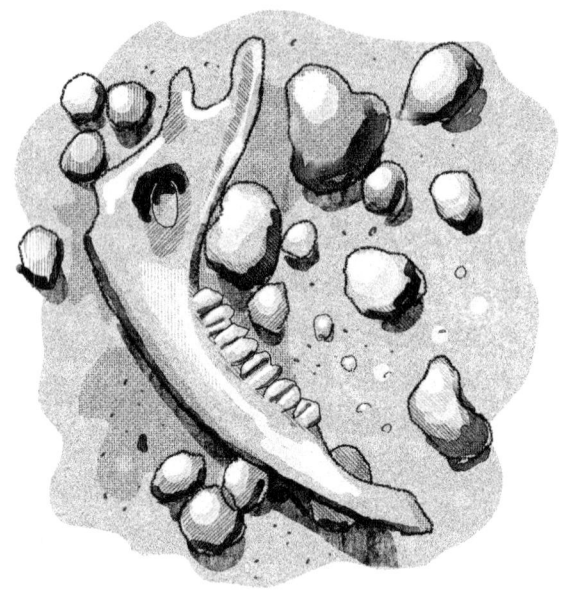

Bones

Charts

London Places with mudlark exhibits

London Places with mudlark exhibits	Details
British Museum, Great Russell Street, London WC1B 3DG	Many artefacts retrieved from the Thames are on display in the museum, including the Battersea Shield and the Waterloo Helmet. https://www.britishmuseum.org/
Imperial War Museum, Lambeth Road SE1 6HZ	Displays of weapons, guns, and ammunition that you might find in the river. https://www.iwm.org.uk/
Museum of London	The Museum is closed and due to reopen in 2025 in Smithfield Market. https://www.museumoflondon.org.uk/museum-london
Museum of London Docklands, No 1, West India Quay, Hertsmere Rd E14 4AL	A Georgian sugar warehouse, now home to a museum chronicling London's history as a trading port. https://www.museumoflondon.org.uk/museum-london-docklands
National Maritime Museum Blackheath Avenue, Greenwich SE10 9NF	The museum hosts mudlarking talks and a popup exhibition with displays through Hands on History. The museum is part of Royal Museums, Greenwich, with the Royal Observatory, Cutty Sark and the Queen's House. https://www.rmg.co.uk/national-maritime-museum\

London Places with mudlark exhibits	Details
Southwark Cathedral London Bridge SE1 9DA	Has displays, books and talks on mudlarking as well as walks led by experts. @southwark_cathedral
Victoria and Albert Museum, Cromwell Road SW7 2RL	Exhibitions with fashions showing Medieval pins, shoes, and clothing. Examples of costumes and tableware found in the river. https://www.vam.ac.uk/

Finds from the Thames

This list comes from the finds I have made and things I've seen other mudlarks retrieve. All of these items have been found up and down the foreshore of the Thames.

Dice

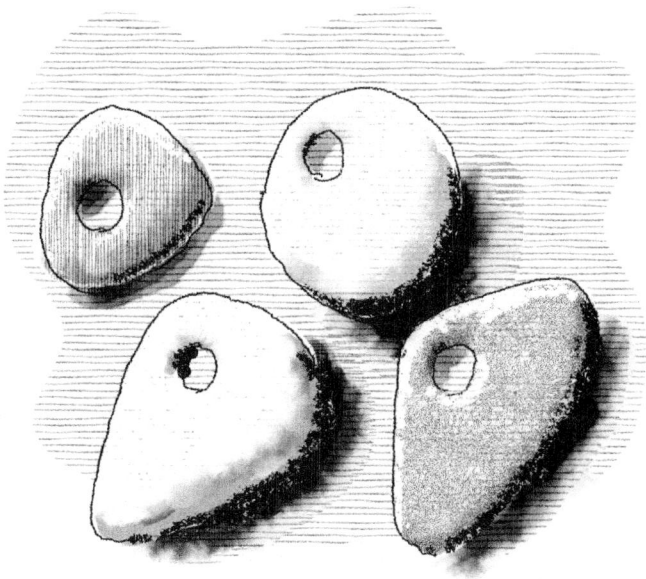

Hagstones

Message in a bottle

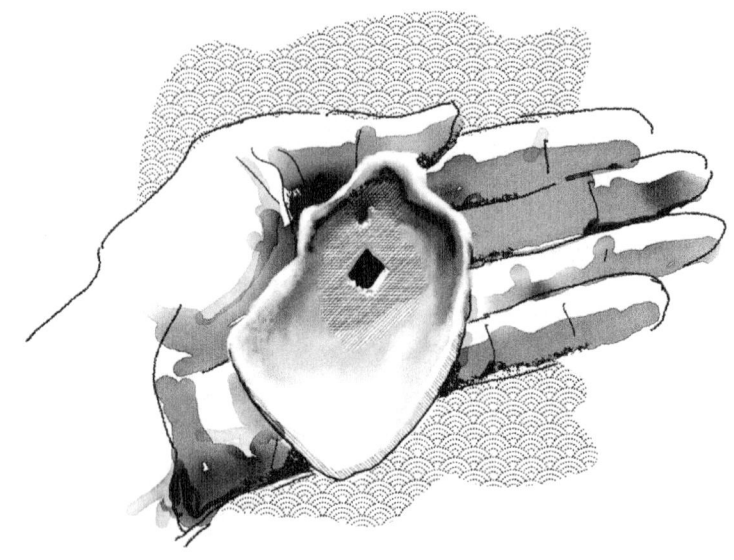

Oyster shell with hole

Finds from the Thames	Description
Beads	People have made and worn beads for thousands of years, and it's hard to date many of the beads people find in the river shingle. They may be made of glass, ceramic, bone, ivory, precious metal, and pearls. Decorative glass beads, sometimes called trade or slave beads, were used between the 16th and 20th centuries as token money for goods, services and enslaved people. Many beads came from Europe, especially Venetian glass chevron beads, which were made in Venice and Murano from the 14th century. Medium rare find.

Finds from the Thames	Description
Bellarmine jug pieces – also called Bartman jugs	Germany exported this stoneware to London in the 16th and 17th centuries, and they were popular for storing wine, beer, ale and even mercury. The brown, shiny surface has a salt glaze, giving it a speckled effect. The decorated bearded faces from the top of the Bellarmine jugs are a special find. Medium rare find.
Bones and teeth	Bones and teeth are probably from butchered animals from long ago. Inform the police if you find human remains. There are many types and sizes of animal bones and teeth on the riverbank. Try to work out which creature they belong to. Pinner bones are an expert find. Easy to find.
Bottles and glass shards	Glass bottles used for wine, beer, medicine, perfume and mineral water can be found in the Thames, even from Roman times. Avoid touching sharp shards, and be careful when emptying strange liquids from sealed bottles. Glass torpedo bottles are a rare find with rounded bases so they had to be stored on their sides so the cork didn't dry out. You'll find plenty of glass shards of lemonade, soda and even gin bottles on the riverbed, thrown away from long-ago picnics. Some bottles still have their corks or stoppers in place. Easy to find.
Bricks	You'll find plenty of red and yellow bricks on the foreshore as London has been rebuilt so many times and bits from demolished buildings got thrown into the river. Look for bricks with letters and numbers in. Easy to find.

Finds from the Thames	Description
Carnelian and coral	Carnelian are orange stones found on the foreshore that were semi-precious gemstones. Coral chunks may have been used as ballast in merchant sailing ships and dumped on the foreshore when they docked. Ballast stopped ships with heavy sails from tipping over. Medium rare find.
Chalk lumps	Chalk does not naturally occur on the foreshore and was used to protect the barges from damage from sharp stones. Amongst the chalk, you may find flints and fossils such as corals and sea urchins. Easy to find.
Clay pipes and stems	Clay pipes are smoking pipes made from clay and are popular finds on the foreshore. The pipe stems are easier to find than the pipe bowls, which can be decorated in beautiful patterns. Pipes were made in Europe from the 16th century after the arrival of tobacco which came to Britain from America in the 1580s. The earliest pipe bowls were small because tobacco was rare and very expensive. If clay pipes are hidden in the mud, they are sometimes completely black, but this colouration can fade within days of contact with the air. Easy to find.

Finds from the Thames	Description
Coins, tokens, and tallies	Remember the saying – 'See a penny, pick it up, and all the day, you'll have good luck'. It's a promising start to the day. Mudlarks find coins with metal detectors, but some can be seen with eyes only. Rare coins from Roman times from 1,500 years ago have been found on the riverbank. Traders produced their metal tokens when the Mint ran out of coins, which they substituted when legal money was in short supply or as a record of promised payments and services. A token can show the trader's name, trade, address and value. Coins and tokens get easier to find when you have learned to get your eye in. Get help by watching an expert. Quite hard to find.
Die or dice	Die or dice from Roman to Post-Medieval times were made from bone, ceramics and wood. Antlers were often used for large bone dice, as they are dense and good for carving. You need to get down on your knees to search for these tiny things. Hard to find.
Doves Press font	One hundred and fifty pieces of the Doves Press font typeface were salvaged from the river in 2014. They were thrown off Hammersmith Bridge in 1917 after a dispute between the owners of the Doves Press publishing company. See the story later. The Super Sewer, Tideway, has commissioned the Doves Type for the lettering on their walls, railings, paving, and ventilation columns. It was first revealed on the Putney Tideway platform in 2023. Very, very rare to find.

Finds from the Thames	Description
Flint tools – axes, arrowheads	Londoners used flints 10,000 years ago, so if you find one, it's rare and ancient. Flint is hard, and its edges can be sharp and made into cutting tools, axes, arrowheads and adzes. The flint is chipped by knapping with a hammer tool to remove flakes and make a sharp edge. A worked flint shows signs of ripples where the blow struck. These Mesolithic, Middle Stone Age tools were used for hunting and cutting up animals. Rare find.
Fossils	Fossils found on the Thames foreshore include ammonites, belemnites, and bivalves, types of marine animals that lived around 85 million years ago. Echinoid fossils are sea urchins fossilised in the flint, which lived between 35–100 million years ago. Folk tradition believed that sea urchin fossils were thunderbolts, able to ward off harm by lightning or witchcraft. They were sometimes placed in Medieval ovens to encourage bread to rise. Rare to find!
Frozen Charlottes	These are tiny porcelain 19th century dolls with a weird story. Charlotte was a young American girl who refused to dress warmly on a winter sleigh ride and froze to death. Children were given this doll sometimes with the message 'Don't be vain and listen to your mother'. The porcelain figures were usually naked and resembled a white corpse. Sometimes, they were baked in cakes, and if you got that slice, it brought you good luck. It's a wonder these dolls survived for a hundred years in the turbulence of the river. Male dolls are called Frozen Charlies. Hard to find.

Finds from the Thames	Description
Garnets	No one knows how semi-precious garnet stones arrived on the riverbank. In the sunshine, they shine bright red like pomegranate seeds in the shingle and are a magical find. They are thought to have come to London for trading and may have been dropped overboard from ships, but their real origin is a mystery. Used in jewellery and as an abrasive for industrial cleaning. Tricky to find, and you need tweezers!
Glass bottles	Pieces of glass bottles are common finds on the riverbank, and people drinking by the river today still throw in beer bottles and glasses from pubs and bars. Apothecary and medicinal bottles, bottles for mineral waters and inks were all made from glass. Easy find.
Hag stones	These are stones with holes all the way through, and for good luck, hang one on your front door to keep out evil spirits. Sailors hung them on their ships to keep out witches and prevent storms. Attach one to your bed to stop bad dreams. The hole in the middle is a portal to fairyland. Easy find.
Human remains	All human remains must be reported to the police and the Museum of London. People have found human skulls, leg and arm bones and human teeth on the foreshore. Rare to find.

Finds from the Thames	Description
Jewellery	Modern and ancient jewellery are found on the Thames foreshore, and mudlarks have discovered rings, necklaces and bracelets thrown into the river, perhaps after an argument or as an offering. Valuable jewellery from over 300 years ago may be considered a treasure if it is made from gold or silver. Gold is a precious metal, and old gold items qualifying as treasure have to be reported. Moderately difficult to find.
Lead cloth seals	In the 17th century, these seals were attached to textile cloth to show the quality and that the taxes had been paid. Quite hard to find.
Messages in bottles	It's fun to find a message in a bottle, but take care if you pick it up, as the contents may not be safe to handle. If you open the bottle, dispose of any liquid safely. Rare to find.
Mother-of-pearl shards	Mother-of-pearl buttons were made from pearl oyster shells cut into discs, polished and pierced. The shells from oysters were imported from the colonies, and London became the centre of the world's trade in mother-of-pearl buttons, and famous for the Pearly Kings and Queens. You find mother-of-pearl shards and sometimes buttons on the river bank. Moderately difficult to find.

Finds from the Thames	Description
Nails and metal stuff	Along the riverbank, plenty of ships were constructed and destroyed in the old shipbuilding areas, and you will find rivets, nails and pieces of metal in these areas. Old nails have the crow's foot mark or 'broad arrow' used since the 14th century to indicate that the nails are the property of the crown. Old nails were made of iron or copper, and you'll find handmade nails on the riverbank, where people made and repaired boats. Easy to find.
Nit combs	Tudor nit combs were made of bone or wood, one side looked like a hair comb, and the other side had finer teeth to comb out nits. Many people in those times had head lice, so these combs were in most households. Rare find.
NOS (nitrous oxide) canisters and Creamers	Shiny, silver-coloured canisters litter parts of the foreshore where people gather. They contain nitrous oxide gas, also known as laughing gas and give users a short high. Creamers are large canisters used for whipping cream and are also filled with nitrous oxide gas, which is inhaled from balloons. Plenty in the river. The government is banning the sale of these items. Sadly, they are quite easy to find.

Finds from the Thames	Description
Oyster shells	Oysters were once the food of the poor, and they were eaten in the taverns along the river. The shells were thrown away and often ended up in the river for us to find. How is it that some have round holes and others have square holes? Holes could be natural, drilled to make buttons, or maybe proof that the owner has paid for something like a trip across the Thames. Discuss and decide. Did the London Oyster Card get its name from these holey shells? That's a great story. Easy things to find.
Pilgrim badges	Pilgrims bought badges made from lead and copper as souvenirs to decorate their clothing or hats after going on a Christian pilgrimage to a holy shrine such as Canterbury Cathedral. The River Thames was considered sacred in Medieval England, so maybe pilgrims threw their badges in the water to express gratitude for their safe journey. However, researchers think they may have been thrown away as rubbish or accidentally lost. The most common pilgrim souvenirs found in London are from Thomas Becket's shrine at Canterbury Cathedral. Very rare to find.

Finds from the Thames	Description
Pins, sewing things and buttons.	'See a pin, pick it up, and all the day you'll have good luck' is an old saying. Does it bring good fortune when mudlarking? If I start my day with a pin, I'm very pleased. Metal pins can often be found in parts of the foreshore where people crossed the river, preserved in the anaerobic mud of the Thames. The shank of the pin was sharpened, and the metal head soldered to the top and often made by children. Pins held together cloaks and scarves and pinned the neck ruffs of Queen Elizabeth and her courtiers. Tudor women wore up to 700 pins a day in their clothes and hair, and royalty wore thousands. Tiny, fine pins were used to pin veils and are hard to find. In Tudor times and later, pins were hand-made from brass, bone, and ivory and have been found on the foreshore. The phrase 'pin money' may have originated during the 14th to 17th centuries when men gave money to the women in their households to buy pins. Women in the 16th century often hung a sewing kit from their belts, including needles, pins, thimbles, dress hooks, and fasteners, and mudlarks have found some on the foreshore. Early buttons had a shank or loop so they could be sewn to the garment. Pins are quite easy to find.

Finds from the Thames	Description
Pinner's bone	Pinner's Bones or Pinholders were usually made from the lower leg of a cow or horse, sawn in half with grooves. The drawn wire was placed in the grooves at the end of the bone at an angle and rotated to sharpen to a pinpoint. The coiled or solid pin head was soldered on afterwards. Before buttons were widely used, rich and poor people were pinned into their clothing, which is why mudlarks find so many pins in the river. Very rare to find.
Posy ring	Posy rings got their name from the word 'posy' or 'posey' based on the French word 'poésy' to describe a motto or poem inscribed inside a ring. From late Medieval times, they had a message for lovers inside, such as 'Your faithful wife during life'. You can buy a replica posy ring at Shakespeare's Globe Theatre shop. Very rare to find.
Pottery pieces – Delftware, Willow Pattern china	Many tiny pieces of discarded pottery are found on the shoreline. Delftware is tin-glazed earthenware named after Delft, the Dutch town, and made in early Medieval times. Popular in Britain from 1650 to 1750, the pieces are often white with blue-painted designs. Delftware includes pottery objects such as plates, ornaments, and tiles. You'll find plenty of pieces of china decorated with transfer prints of the Blue Willow Pattern, which became popular for dinner services in 18th century Britain. The pattern copied the hand-painted blue and white porcelain imported from China. Quite easy to find.

Finds from the Thames	Description
Sacred things	Over the years, many things have been thrown into the river as faith offerings. For hundreds of years, pilgrims' badges, bells, and ampullae have been found in the River Thames, probably thrown in the water for religious reasons. The Battersea Shield was an offering made to the River Thames by Celtic tribes hundreds of years ago. In 1970, the Thames was blessed to become another sacred river. Moderately easy to find.
Shellfish – clams, mussels	Small clam shells pile along the foreshore, probably the Asian clam (Corbicula fluminea), which invaded British waters in 1998. Why has this clam population increased? It's probably because the Thames is so much cleaner. The zebra mussel is another invasive species. Easy to find.
Shoes	Anything made from leather will decompose in water unless it is buried in the river mud, where the lack of oxygen delays decay. Mudlarks take special care in preserving old leather shoes to discover how they were made. Old shoes are a rare find.
Slipware	Slipware is decorated, lead-glazed earthenware. The yellow glazed pieces have brown lines of slip combed through like feathering an iced cake. The slip is loose clay and water mixed into a creamy consistency in a contrasting colour to the body of the vessel. By the mid-1600s, potteries produced large quantities of domestic items decorated with slipware designs, and you'll find sherds of slipware all along the Thames. Quite easy to find.

Finds from the Thames	Description
Spongeware	Spongeware was made in Staffordshire potteries in the 1750s and was popular for domestic ware into the 19th century. The patterns were applied by hand using specially cut sponges so each piece is unique. Quite easy to find.
Sugar cones or moulds	Sherds of red unglazed pottery sugar cones, with white streaks of glaze on the inside, appeared along the Thames, and they were used to produce sugar loaves. Sugar was a luxury until the 18th century, and the moulds held hot sugar as it crystallised, drained and cooled into an expensive sugar loaf. Moderately easy to find.
Tiles with paw prints	Some say that the tile maker would deliberately leave tiles and bricks out to dry where paw prints could be made by passing cats, dogs and other animals. These tiles were thought to bring luck and could sell for a higher price. They were sometimes used on the tiled entrance of Georgian houses. Finding one of these is rare and special.
Tin-glazed earthenware (delftware or delft)	Tin-glazed earthenware, known also as delftware or delft, was the first white pottery manufactured in Britain. Chinese porcelain in the Post-Medieval period was costly, so locally made delft took its place. The white surface is made by mixing tin oxide into the glaze. In the 16th and 17th centuries, Holland and Britain became centres of tin glaze production. Pots were fired unglazed – called biscuit firing – before submerging in liquid glaze and dried. The second kiln firing fused the glaze to the pot. Patterns could be drawn in different colours on the white glaze. Quite easy to find.

Finds from the Thames	Description
Tudor money boxes	These green-glazed money boxes were used in London theatres in Elizabethan times, and the coins for tickets were posted through a slit in the side. When the pot was full, it had to be broken to get the payment out. Mudlarks find the tops of these pots, called knops, on the riverbank. When the Museum of London Archaeology (MOLA) excavated the Rose Theatre in 1988 and 2010, they uncovered lots of Tudor money box pieces. A complete one is on display in the British Museum. Popular between 1300-1600. Knops are found on Bankside near the theatres. The Museum of London has nearly 200 money pots. Rare to find.
Vapes	Multicoloured plastic vapes get dumped in the Thames and washed up on the foreshore. Some contain lithium-ion batteries, which can cause fires. One burnt a hole in my pocket after I picked it up from the riverbank. 2023 News – the UK government wants to ban vapes as they are causing littering and are a fire hazard. Five million disposable vapes are thrown away each week in the UK, but few are recycled. They could be mudlark treasures of the future. Sadly, they are easy to find.
Vulcanite stoppers	Black vulcanite bottle stoppers are made from hardened rubber and used to seal bottles of beer, ginger beer, and fizzy water. Invented in 1872, they are sometimes decorated with images and letters to show the company name. Moderately hard to find.

Clam shells

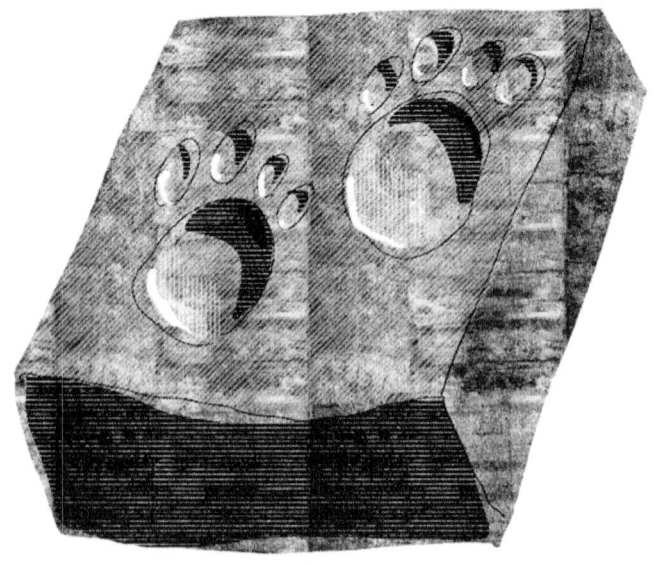

Paw print on tile

Vulcanite stoppers

Wildlife in the Thames

Wander along the Thames foreshore, and you'll notice so much wildlife that inhabits stretches of the river. Ducks, geese, and swans swim on the water and waddle on the shore, herons stand stock still waiting for fish, and flights of birds skim overhead, using the river as a migration route during the spring and autumn. The river seems to be getting cleaner in some areas, and seagulls and cormorants dive down to feed, but who knows with the regular dumps of waste sewage into the water. Long ago, the river was a rich food source of fish, eels, and oysters but in the populated area of the city, the pollution is too high.

This chart describes some of the wildlife you find as you mudlark. After the Tideway Super Sewer has opened and the old storm drains that push overflow into the Thames have been capped, hopefully, the water quality will improve, and more wildlife will return.

Wildlife in the Thames	Description
Birds – cormorants, crows, grey herons, seagulls, and swans	There are plenty of birds that live and fly beside the river. Black cormorants perch on rocks and boats, flapping and drying their vast wings after they dive to fish in the river. On the foreshore, rooks tear the plump insides of clam shells with their beaks, and grey herons stand still in the water, watching for prey. Plenty of seagulls fish in the river and feed off tourist bread, along with ducks and geese who bring up their young in the river reeds. The huge white swans mate for life, so it is a happy sight to see a pair swimming with their cygnets on the river and a real experience as the group fly overhead in a V-shaped formation.
Crustaceans – crabs, crayfish and shrimps	The Chinese Mitten Crab, Eriocheir Sinensis, is an invasive species found along the foreshore and first recorded in 1935. In large numbers, they can block and damage water outlets and riverbanks and were thought to have arrived in ships ballast. You'll find them on the riverbank, alive, dead, as well as their empty, discarded exoskeletons. Several crayfish species live in the river – native white-clawed crayfish, the introduced Signal crayfish, and the endangered Noble crayfish. Small, transparent shrimps can be found on the edges of the foreshore, and you can see them when you turn over stones at the water's edge. Do not eat crustaceans and fish from the river due to pollution.

Wildlife in the Thames	Description
Ducks and geese	Many varieties of ducks live on the Thames – mallard, shoveller, mandarin. Different geese, too – Brent geese, Canada geese, Egyptian geese. These birds can be noisy during the breeding season in early summer as they protect their young and grumble and quack when mudlarks disturb them.
Eels	The European eel found in the Thames is critically endangered due to habitat destruction, barriers such as weirs, which prevent their migration, and overfishing. European eels are born in the Sargasso Sea and swim over 5,000 km to estuaries, such as the Thames. Years ago, eels were a cheap, nutritious, and readily available food for the people of London, but they are not popular today. Eel numbers in the Thames have dropped massively in recent years.
Fish	Freshwater fish found in the Thames today include bream, pike and carp. Seawater fish in the Thames Estuary include trout, flounder, pike, salmon, roach, perch, barbel, chub, and carp. The main river through the city is too polluted to catch fish to eat.
Oysters	There are few wild native oyster populations in the UK, but some are farmed in the outer Thames Estuary. Oysters are useful to the environment as they clean the water where they live. The English southeast coast has been home to oyster beds and fisheries for centuries and even supplied the Romans with oysters.

Wildlife in the Thames	Description
Seals and Sharks	Grey and harbour seals live in the Thames Estuary and sometimes swim upriver towards London. Five shark species are found in the Thames Estuary, including Tope and Starry Smoothhound sharks.
Shellfish	You'll find shells from oysters, mussels, clams, whelks, and winkles on the riverbank. Most shells surveyed from the Thames are two invasive species – the Zebra Mussel and the Asian Clam, enjoyed by seagulls, rooks and crows. Mussel numbers in the Thames have dropped by 95% in recent years. Don't eat the shellfish from the river due to pollution.
Short-snouted Seahorse – Hippocampus Hippocampus	Young seahorses were found in 2017 at Greenwich, and mudlarks have discovered their dried skeletons on the foreshore. They grow to 15cm to 17cm and live in shallow, coastal waters amongst the rocks in the warmer months of the year. The males of the species get pregnant and give birth – the only known species to do this. I'd love to find one.
Whale – The River Thames Whale	Affectionately nicknamed Willy by Londoners, this juvenile female northern bottlenose whale was found swimming in the Thames near Battersea Bridge in January 2006. Sadly, Willy died after a rescue attempt

Charts

Mitten crab

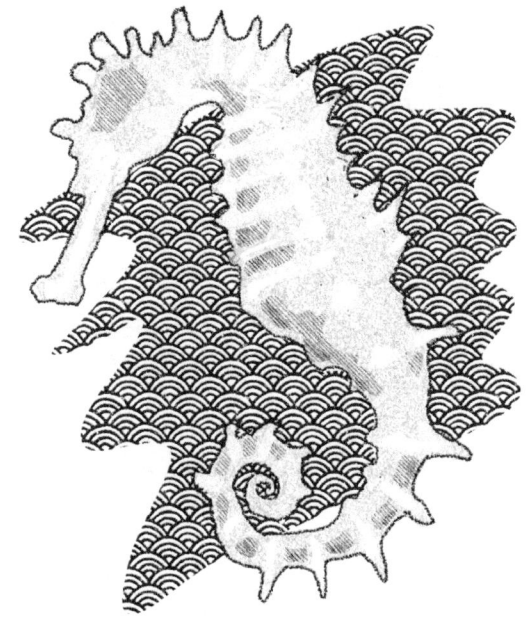

Seahorse

Useful Contacts

These are websites for organisations that are involved with the Thames.

Useful Contacts	Website address
Canoe London	Has a useful document on Thames access from 2013. Be aware that some steps and access points have closed since then. https://canoelondon.com/wordpress/wp-content/uploads/2013/04/Access-to-the-River-Thames.pdf
City Cruises London – river cruises	You can hop between river piers with a single ticket or take in a round tour with their 24-hour River Pass. https://www.cityexperiences.com/london/city-cruises/
Finds Liaison Officer (FLO)	Take special historic finds to FLO https://www.museumoflondon.org.uk/contact-us
Foreshore Recording and Observation Group(FROGs)	Over 700 volunteers are trained in foreshore recording techniques and foreshore health and safety. They record the archaeology of the Thames foreshore and help research the history of the river. http://www.thamesdiscovery.org/frog-blog/
Fossil beds	Abbey Wood Fossil Beds are open for public digging with permission with fossils of shark's teeth, fish, mammal, and bird remains. The fossil pit is near Lesnes Abbey, a former abbey now in ruins. Shark's teeth are the most common find. Take a mesh sieve, container, sample bags, tweezers, and a basin for washing samples. Parksandopenspaces@bexley.gov.uk 02083037777 It's a Site of Special Scientific Interest SSSI.

Useful Contacts	Website address
FROG	FROG members monitor, record, and research the archaeology of the Thames foreshore across London. http://www.thamesdiscovery.org/frog-blog/
Historic England	Lists sites of historical interest and the website has lots of research into local history. https://historicengland.org.uk/
John Rocque's 1746 map of London	A 24-sheet plan of the cities of London and Westminster, and Borough of Southwark, surveyed by John Rocque and engraved by John Pine. This map created between 1737 and 1746 is useful for research, locating historical areas of London in the 18th century. https://www.locatinglondon.org/static/Rocque.html
Juerg's London	A useful website of areas around the river with grid references and nice pubs. http://www.juerg.co.uk/london
Know your London	A great website created by Adrian Prockter, who was a lecturer specialising in Inner London. Really useful to discover the history of London, especially the city area and the River Thames. https://knowyourlondon.wordpress.com/
Layers of London	A map-based history website developed by the Institute of Historical Research. Users can access free historical maps of London and contribute stories, memories, and histories to create a social history resource about their area. https://www.layersoflondon.org/

Useful Contacts	Website address
Lionheart Replicas	This company is run by Colin and Colleen Torode, who are experts on making replica historical pewter for things like pilgrim badges. https://www.lionheartreplicas.co.uk
London Fire Brigade	Information on river safety. https://www.london-fire.gov.uk/safety/water-safety/
London Waterkeeper	London Waterkeeper is a member of Waterkeeper® Alliance, focusing on citizen action on issues that affect our waterways. www.londonwaterkeeper.org.uk
Museum of London Archaeology (MOLA)	An experienced and innovative archaeology and built-heritage practice. https://www.mola.org.uk
The Museum of London Docklands	Mudlarks is an interactive space for our younger visitors and their carers. Look up information on their collections. https://www.museumoflondon.org.uk/museum-london-docklands Museum of London closed 2022. Moving to Smithfield General Market from 2026.
Portable Antiquities Scheme (PAL)	PAL records all archaeological finds made by the public in England and Wales. If your finds count as treasure, contact the coroner for the district, usually within fourteen days of making the find. The Treasure Act code of practice contains a directory of coroners in the Thames area. (https://finds.org.uk/)
Uber River Bus	Running between Putney and North Woolwich, this is an easy way to get about on the river and spot access down to mudlarking sites and beaches. https://tfl.gov.uk/modes/river/about-river-bus

Useful Contacts	Website address
Southwark Cathedral Mudlarking and the walks	Occasional mudlark displays, exhibitions and walks. The shop sells things relating to mudlarking. https://southwarkcathedralshop.org/collections/mudlarking https://cathedral.southwark.anglican.org/whats-on/river-thames-foreshore-walks-22-july-23/
Thames 21	Thames21 has over 7000 volunteers for waterway improvement activities across London every year such as the Big Wet Wipe survey. https://www.thames21.org.uk/
Thames Barrier	One of the largest movable flood barriers in the world run by the Environment Agency. https://www.gov.uk/guidance/the-thames-barrier
Thames Discovery Programme	A community archaeology project promoting and protecting the Thames foreshore heritage in London. Public walks are organised. Records and monitors the archaeology on the Thames foreshore and gets Londoners involved and hands-on with their heritage. http://www.thamesdiscovery.org/
Thames Explorer Trust	River education along the tidal Thames with walks. https://thames-explorer.org.uk/
Thames Festival Trust	A diverse programme of events with the River Thames as its centrepiece. https://thamesfestivaltrust.org/

Useful Contacts	Website address
Thames River Trust	A charity focused on improving the ecosystem of the Thames and its tributaries. https://www.thamesriverstrust.org.uk/ Fantastic map of fish migration. https://www.thamesriverstrust.org.uk/thames-catchment-community-eels-project/rivers-fish-migration/
Thames Tides Tidal Thames Tide Times Easytide – tide prediction	http://thamestides.org.uk/todayp http://tidalthames.co.uk/ https://www.tidetimes.org.uk/ https://easytide.admiralty.co.uk/?PortID=
Thames Tideway Tunnel	London's new Super Sewer, due to be completed in 2025 and costing £3.9bn, is designed to capture more than 95% of the sewage spills. https://www.tideway.london/
Thames Water real-time sewer overflow map	This map provides near real-time information about storm overflow activity, as indicated by event duration monitoring. https://www.thameswater.co.uk/edm-map
The Agas Map	Birds-eye view of London, first printed from woodblocks in about 1561 with details of buildings and streets in the City. Prepared by MoEML (Map of Early and Modern London) https://mapoflondon.uvic.ca/map.htm

Useful Contacts	Website address
The Port of London Authority – (PLA permits)	Rules on using the foreshore with permits – http://www.pla.co.uk/Environment/Thames-foreshore-permits PLA Permit boundary – The permit is not valid east of the Thames Barrier, and no searching/digging is allowed on the foreshore of the River Thames east of this point. PLA and metal detectors. https://www.pla.co.uk/Environment/Thames-foreshore-access-including-metal-detecting-searching-and-digging Map showing areas with no searching or digging. https://gis.pla.co.uk/portal/apps/webappviewer/index.html?id=5f5f552365114082963ad4ffb3a6b17f
The Rivers Trust	Provides information on sewage and storm discharge into rivers. www.theriverstrust.org/
The Thames Path	A 184-mile long-distance footpath from the source of the River Thames in Tewksbury Mead, Gloucestershire, to the Thames Barrier in Woolwich, London. The path gives access to much of the foreshore on either side of the river in central London. https://www.nationaltrail.co.uk/en_GB/trails/thames-path/
Totally Thames	Holds an annual celebration of the River Thames – usually in September. Walk along the Thames to see large-scale art installations, free exhibitions and live performances and join an archaeological tour of the river's surroundings. https://www.mola.org.uk/totally-thames-guided-walks

Useful Contacts	Website address
Wandle News	A website designed by Olivia, with information on how to get down to the riverbank with clear photos and descriptions of findings. https://wandlenews.com/beaches-on-the-thames/
Zoological Society	Carries out regular, valuable research on the animals that live in the Thames. https://www.zsl.org

Places with food, drink and great river views

Many places are free to visit, and you can look over The Thames and view the beaches and the busy river traffic and spot areas to mudlark. It's great to see how the river curves and swirls through the City from the sky-high viewing places. When the river is at low tide you can see how wide the foreshore is and spot the mudlarks in their favourite spots.

Places with food, drink and great river views	Description
12th Knot at Sea Containers, Upper Ground, South Bank SE1 9PD	Book one of the terrace tables for river views. Look over to the cityscape and view St. Pauls, Millennium Bridge and the beach of Queenhithe. Great at night when London, and especially the river bridges, sparkles with lights.
Battersea Power Station Chimney Lift 109, Battersea SW11 8BJ	Go to Lift 109 and travel up the chimney 109 metres to the top for 360-degree views of London's skyline, east towards the city and west to Putney and Hammersmith. Great for spotting mudlarking areas around Chelsea and Battersea.

Places with food, drink and great river views	Description
Bokan, 40 Marsh Wall, Canary Wharf E14 9TP	Restaurant 39th floor of the Novotel London Canary Wharf.
Browns, Butlers Wharf, 26 Shad Thames, London SE1 2YG	All-day brasserie and bar with lobster nights and afternoon tea in a grand café setting with tables overlooking the river.
Butlers Wharf Chop House, 36e Shad Thames, London SE1 2PJ	A menu of chophouse classics, steaks and nostalgic British recipes, plus Tower Bridge and River Thames views.
Coppa Club, Tower Bridge, 3 Three Quays Walk, Lower Thames St, EC3R 6AH	Riverside terrace with private igloos looking over the river near The Tower of London.
Coq D'Argent, 1 Poultry, City of London, EC2R 8EJ	Panoramic views from rooftop terraces for meals and drinks.
Doggett's Coat and Badge Pub, Blackfriars Bridge, South Bank SE1 9UD	Thomas Doggett organised the London Bridge to Chelsea rowing race in 1715 on the Thames. The winner was given the Doggett's Coat and Badge, and this pub is named after the race.
Emirates Air Line Cable Car, 27 Western Gateway, E16 1FA	The IFS Cloud Cable Car crosses the Thames between Greenwich Peninsula and the Royal Docks. Travel 1 kilometre over the Thames, 10 minutes each way, with unique city views, 90 metres above the river so you can plan your mudlark walks.

Places with food, drink and great river views	Description
Founders Arms, 52 Hopton St, London SE1 9JH	A glass-fronted pub with a large, heated patio overlooking the River Thames and St Paul's. Great fish and chips with mushy peas and views of the river beaches. Watch famous mudlarks trudging along in their Wellies as they come off the foreshore.
Heron Tower, Duck and Waffle and Sushisamba, City of London, EC2N 4AY	Very high tower with river views from the restaurants and a free glass lift to access dining areas.
Horizon22, 22 Bishopsgate, London EC2N 4AJ	London's highest free viewing platform with 300-degree views of London and its landmarks.
One New Change, New Change, City of London, EC4M 9AF	Rooftop open-air viewing gallery with views over St. Paul's Cathedral dome. Take a glass-sided elevator to the 6th floor. Free.
OXO Tower Restaurant, Brasserie and Bar, Queens Walk, South Bank SE1 9PH	8th floor of the famous OXO Tower, with incredible views across the Thames. Free, public area with views over the river, St. Paul's, and the city. OXO regularly teams up with Thames21 to remove foreshore plastics.
Rich Stein's, Tideway Yard, 125 Mortlake High St, Mortlake W14 8SW	Great tables overlooking the Thames at Mortlake serving seafood.
Royal Festival Hall, South Bank Centre, Skylon Restaurant SE1 8XX	Wonderful river views from the tables in Skylon restaurant and a cocktail bar.

Places with food, drink and great river views	Description
Salt Quay Pub, Rotherhithe, 163 Rotherhithe St SE16 5QU	Salt Quay Pub is an old warehouse-style building on the banks of the river with great views down to Rotherhithe.
Sky Garden, 1, Sky Garden Walk, City of London EC3M 8AF	Top of the Walkie Talkie building on the 35th floor, a covered garden, and balcony views from the North Bank of the river. Book a free ticket in advance.
St. Paul's Cathedral Dome, City of London EC4M 8AD	Hundreds of steps up to a narrow walkway around the outside of the Dome with an entry ticket.
Swan at The Globe, 21 New Globe Walk, Bankside, London SE1 9DT	Modern riverside bar and restaurant, linked to Shakespeare's Globe Theatre, with Thames views.
Tate Modern 6th floor, Bankside SE1 9TG	Great views over the Thames to St Paul's Cathedral and the Millenium Bridge. Spot the mudlarks down on the beach below Trig Lane Stairs. You can eat there too. It's free to see the view, but you need to ask permission.
Thames Barrier Information Centre, 1 Unity Way, Woolwich SE18 5NJ	The Barrier spans the River Thames near Woolwich and protects London from flooding by tidal surges. You need to book ahead to visit.
The Angel Pub, Bermondsey Wall SE16 4NB	This is a traditional riverside pub with views over the river and Rotherhithe beach.
The Blacksmiths Arms, 257 Rotherhithe St SE16 5EJ	A pub with a small sitting area at the back, overlooking the river.

Places with food, drink and great river views	Description
The Captain Kidd Pub, 108 Wapping High St E1W 2NE	The pub is named after the 17th century pirate William Kidd, who was executed at Execution Dock. The pub is near old steps leading down to the river and has outdoor seating.
The Cutty Sark Pub, 4-6 Ballast Quay, Greenwich SE10 9PD	A Georgian riverside pub over three floors, with Thames views of The O2 arena from the dining room.
The Gun Pub, Coldharbour, Docklands E14 9NS	Terrace overlooks the river and The O2 arena with one of the best views in London.
The London Eye, Westminster Bridge Road SE1 7PB	Spend time in a capsule with other tourists high up with views of the Thames to the east and west so you can map out your trips.
The Mayflower Pub, Rotherhithe SE16 4NF	Views over the Thames from the balcony where the Mayflower boat left for America. Rickety steps to the side of the pub with a challenging descent down to the beach.
The Monument, City of London EC4R 9AA	Book a ticket and climb 311 narrow steps up a spiral staircase for views from the 61-metre column built to commemorate The Great Fire of London in 1666. The Monument has a shiny golden dome and stands high above the surrounding buildings. Mudlark on the river foreshore nearby and find a brick or tile from that time, perhaps with scorch marks from the fire.
The Mudlark Pub, South Bank SE1 9DA	No river view but famous with mudlarks. Named after the 18th century practice of scavenging in the mud for things to sell from the Thames.

Places with food, drink and great river views	Description
The Old Thameside Inn, Pickfords Wharf, Clink St, London SE1 9DG	Riverside pub has exposed brickwork and flagstone floors and a large terrace with panoramic views.
The Oystershed, 1 Angel Lane EC4R 3AB	A bright riverside bar with stripped floors and huge windows for seafood and classic British dishes. Situated on the North Bank with views over the river.
The Prospect of Whitby, 64 Wapping Wall, Wapping E1W 3SH	One of London's oldest riverside pubs dating back to 1520 and the balcony on the first floor overlooks the river. Haunt for smugglers, thieves, and pirates. Climb down Pelican Steps in an alley beside the pub, leading to Wapping Beach and views over to Execution Dock.
The River Café, Thames Wharf, Rainville Rd, London W6 9HA	Inventive seasonal Italian cuisine and fine wines in an airy riverside location with outdoor dining. You need to book as it's so popular. One of my favourites.
The Samuel Pepys, Stew Lane, City of London EC4V 3PT	Overlooking Queenhithe and the river, the balcony is a great place for spotting mudlarks at work, especially at night.
The Shard, 32 London Bridge St SE1 9SG	Aqua Shard on level 31, has panoramic views of the oldest parts of the Thames. It's tricky to get in without a booking.
The Trafalgar Tavern, Park Row, Greenwich SE10 9NW	Overlooking Greenwich Beach. During Queen Victoria's reign, it was frequented by Charles Dickens.

Places with food, drink and great river views	Description
The Windjammer Pub, 25 Admiralty Ave, Newham E16 2PN	A smart pub overlooking Pontoon Dock and the Thames Barrier.
Tower Bridge, Tower Bridge Rd SE1 2UP	Walk across Tower Bridge roadway for free. Buy a ticket to the upper-level Glass Floor Walkway, 42 metres above the river. Amazing views up and down to great mudlarking beaches.
Town of Ramsgate Pub, 62 Wapping High St, Wapping E1W 2PN	The pub has a terrace overlooking the river, and Hanging Judge Jeffreys was caught outside as he was trying to flee in 1688. Wapping Old Stairs leads down to a nearby beach with a gruesome history of executing pirates by drowning.

Thames places to visit

These places all have links to The Thames foreshore and are interesting for researching your finds and discovering their history.

Thames places to visit	Details
British Museum Great Russell Street, London WC1B 3DG	Home to the Portable Antiquities Scheme with its online database. View The Battersea Shield found in the Thames from the Iron Age. https://www.britishmuseum.org/

Thames places to visit	Details
Brunel Museum Railway Avenue Rotherhithe, SE16 4LF	Brunel's Thames Tunnel once provided a pedestrian crossing of the River Thames nearly two miles downstream of London Bridge. Guided tours into the shaft. https://thebrunelmuseum.com
Crossness Pumping Station Bazalgette Way Abbey Wood SE2 9AQ	A Victorian sewer system that continues to serve the capital. https://www.crossness.org.uk/
Imperial War Museum, Lambeth Road SE1 6HZ	Displays of weapons, guns, and ammunition that people sometimes find in the river. https://www.iwm.org.uk/
Museum of London Docklands, No 1, West India Quay, Hertsmere Rd E14 4AL	Georgian sugar warehouse, now home to a museum chronicling London's history as a trading port. https://www.museumoflondon.org.uk/museum-london-docklands Museum of London (closed 2023 due to reopen in 2025 in Smithfield Market)
The National Army Museum, Royal Hospital Road, Chelsea London SW3 4HT	The National Army Museum Collection is the world's largest collection of objects and archives relating to the British Army. https://www.nam.ac.uk/
National Maritime Museum, Blackheath Avenue, Greenwich SE10 8XJ	Situated within a Unesco World Heritage Site, the museum is part of Royal Museums Greenwich, which includes the Royal Observatory, Cutty Sark, and the Queen's House. Hosts mudlarking talks and a popup exhibition with displays through Hands on History. https://www.rmg.co.uk/national-maritime-museum\

Thames places to visit	Details
Southwark Cathedral London Bridge SE1 9DA	Displays, books, and talks on mudlarking as well as taking river walks. @southwark_cathedral
The Cutty Sark, King William Walk, London SE10 9HT	The Cutty Sark was the world's last surviving tea clipper and the fastest ship of her time and is now a major London attraction. https://www.rmg.co.uk/cutty-sark
The Thames Barrier Information Centre, 1 Unity Way, Woolwich SE18 5NJ	The Thames Barrier Information Centre has a small exhibition where you can learn about the construction of the Thames Barrier to show how it works. Only pre-booked tours are permitted. https://www.gov.uk/guidance/the-thames-barrier
The Thames River Police Museum in Wapping	A tiny museum visited by appointment only with tales of the Thames River Police, which is the oldest organised police force in existence. http://www.thamespolicemuseum.org.uk/museum.html

Thames Beaches

If you see a beach at low tide along the Thames foreshore, you have probably found a place to mudlark. Check the access and exit routes before you go down.

To find a London beach, type 'London beach' into Google, and a list comes up.

Click the link of the beach and view the uploaded photographs.

Rotherhithe Beach

Thames Beaches	Description
Bankside Beach, 52 Hopton St, London SE1 9JH	Large sandy area in front of Tate Modern and Gabriel's Wharf – easy concrete stairs down.
Bermondsey Beach, Southwark SE16 4TT	Views of city skyscrapers and a wide, sandy, shingly beach to walk along.
Deptford Beach Watergate St, London SE8 3JF	Access is down an alleyway beside the Master Shipwright's House. The stone steps can be slippery. Deptford was the launch area for many colonial and slavery expeditions and the shipyard of the East India Company.
Folly House Beach, Isle of Dogs E1W 1UR	Views from the Isle of Dogs to The O2 arena and Greenwich.
Greenwich Beach, Greenwich SE10 9NW	A long, sandy beach that runs in front of the Old Royal Naval College and has two sets of stairs for access.
Hidden Beach, 1 Fountain Green Square, Bermondsey SE16 4TX	Great view of Tower Bridge – stone stairs descend to the foreshore.

Thames Beaches	Description
OXO Tower Beach, Queens Walk, South Bank SE1 9PH	Long, sandy beach accessible by stairs to the foreshore.
Ratcliff Beach, 12 Narrow St, Ratcliff E14 8DH	Entrance from Narrow Street to a small, sandy beach which is home to a flock of swans fed by locals. Great views of Canary Wharf.
Rotherhithe Beach, Rotherhithe SE16 5QT	Sandy stretch of beach near the Mayflower Pub. Steps off Rotherhithe St.
Royal Victoria Dock E16 1AH	The dock is beneath the Emirates cable car with a watersports centre, offering wakeboarding on the river.
Thames Beach, Queens Walk, Gabriels Wharf SE1 9PP	Right below Gabriels Wharf. Easy access with good stairs. Sand sculptures at low tide.
Tower Beach, Tower of London EC3N 4DT	Closed in 1971, the public is no longer allowed on this beach.
Wapping Beach, Wapping E1W 3SH	Wooden stairs going to a sandy, shingly beach. Use the famous Pelican Stairs to get down.
Waterloo Beach 56 Upper Ground, London SE1 9PP	A sandy beach with easy access to take photos of the City.

Glossary of mudlarking terms

This Glossary shares the new and sometimes strange words that I've learned and helps me communicate better when I've been mudlarking. It's a bit like learning Cockney Rhyming Slang! Climb down the Apple and Pears.

Nightlark

Glossary of mudlarking terms	What does it mean?
Ballast	Ballast was used to weigh down tall ships with heavy masts and stop them from tipping over. Materials for ballast included rocks, gravel, sand, and even pig iron. Interesting fossils arrived on the foreshore with rock ballast from around the world.
Beaches on the Thames	These are places where there's a foreshore at low tide, sometimes with a sandy shoreline and access for mudlarking.
Detectorist	A person whose hobby is using a metal detector to find things in the ground.
Draw Docks	This is an area, creek, or inlet for unloading barges so they can tie up and wait for the tide to go out. Useful for access down to the foreshore but seek permission.

Glossary of mudlarking terms	What does it mean?
Eyes-only search	This means searching the foreshore by just looking, without digging or scraping and not using a metal detector. Some areas of the foreshore, like on the shoreline in front of Queenhithe, are eyes-only search places with no surface disturbance.
Finding lines	Certain materials or fragments tend to rest together along the same finding lines. The waves of the Thames shift and sort objects and deposit them on the foreshore in distinct groups, often by weight. For example, heavier metal pieces like pins, nails, and coins will gather together. Animal bones are lighter, and they collect together in certain areas. Locating a finding line is a useful skill to learn for searching.
Flooding	In 1928, the Thames flooded most of the East End, and hundreds of lives were lost across the east of England. There was another major flood in 1953, which led to the construction of the Thames Barrier. Increasing sea levels mean the Barrier may only protect the city until around 2060.
Frost Fairs	The Thames Frost Fairs were held on the River Thames between 1608 and 1824 during cold winters when the river froze over. People could ice skate, dance, race horses on the thick ice, and buy food and drink from the market stalls. Today's expert mudlarks find trinkets from Frost Fairs, like rings and souvenirs lost in the river all those years ago.

Glossary of mudlarking terms	What does it mean?
Getting your eye in	A term used by mudlarks to show how, if you practise and search for specific shapes, such as circular things, you will find things in the sand and shingle. Circular shapes include rings, coins, pipe bowls and bottle ends. Beginners, like me, can mistake an open clamshell as a pipe bowl, but learn how to progress.
'I eat rubbish' cages	You'll find these cages labelled I eat rubbish, floating in the Thames collecting rubbish such as driftwood and plastic bottles. The PLA recovers up to 300 tonnes of rubbish from these cages every year.
Lightermen and watermen	These people lightened or unloaded a ship and transferred the cargo to another vessel or onto the shore. Since 1700, lightermen and watermen can be members of the same livery company or guild, The Company of Watermen and Lightermen of the River Thames.
Londinium	Londinium was the provincial capital of Roman Britain, established by the Romans in the first century AD. It became a thriving centre of commerce, importing and selling olive oil, wine, pottery, glass and marble. Much of this material was loaded, transported and off-loaded from shipping on the River Thames.

Glossary of mudlarking terms	What does it mean?
Metal detecting	To detect metal along the foreshore using a machine, you need permission. The PLA says, 'All of the foreshore in the UK has an owner. Metal detecting, searching or digging is not a public right, and as such, it needs the permission of the landowner. The PLA and the Crown Estate are the largest land owners of Thames foreshore and jointly administer a permit which allows metal detecting, searching or digging.'
Metal line	Metal pieces, such as screws, nails, old tools, coins, and pins, congregate together on the riverbank in metal lines. Mudlarks like to find a metal line to search for treasure.
Mudlark	A person who made a livelihood by searching for iron, coal, and old ropes in mud or low tide in the 18th century. Today, modern mudlarks search the riverbank for treasure as a hobby and interest in history.
Mudlark Badge	Badge was designed by Sean O'Mara. The image is like a Pirate's Jolly Roger flag with a skull and crossbones, using a mudlark trowel instead of bones. The number 346 is the full length of the Thames in kilometres and the forehead on the skull shows the curve of the River Thames through London. Sean made the badges as a fun project, gave them away to mudlarks on the foreshore and left some behind for others to find. Lucky them!

Glossary of mudlarking terms	What does it mean?
Nightlarking	Mudlarking at night in the dark. Use a head torch to see the foreshore and lark with others for safety. Avoid walking too near deep water on your own or late at night – it's easy to slip and fall in.
Pinch points	These are areas of the Thames Foreshore where the tide comes in faster than expected and risks cutting you off. Look out for the nearest steps, stairs or ladders to get on and off the foreshore and watch out for pinch points.A
Scheduled Ancient Monuments	Historic England describes scheduling as the oldest form of heritage protection, which began in 1913. The 1882 Ancient Monuments Protection Act compiled a list of prehistoric monuments deserving of state protection. Only deliberately created structures, features, and remains can be scheduled. The Roman and Medieval waterfront at Queenhithe Dock is a Scheduled Monument, as is Greenwich Palace foreshore, and Launch Ways of SS Great Eastern. No digging, metal detecting, searching and/or disturbance are allowed. These areas are labelled in red on the PLA river map.
Scraping	Scraping is when the foreshore is disturbed with tools such as rakes or trowels, and it is forbidden on the North Bank between the Millenium Bridge and London Bridge. Permits for other areas allow you to scrape down 7.5cm below the surface of the riverbank.

Glossary of mudlarking terms	What does it mean?
Searching	Searching includes activities such as searching by eye, metal detecting, digging, or scraping. It's done by gently removing the surface of the foreshore.
Shard or sherd?	Shard is used for a fragment of glass, but archaeologists prefer to use the word sherd for fragments of pottery.
Thames Barrier near Woolwich	One of the largest movable flood barriers in the world run by the Environment Agency.
The Boat Race	The Boat Race is an annual rowing race on the River Thames between Oxford and Cambridge Universities and one of the oldest sporting events in the world. Separate men's and women's races cover a 6.8 km (4.2-mile) stretch of the Thames in West London, from Putney to Mortlake.
The Great Fire of London 1666	The Great Fire gutted the City of London and started in a bakery in Pudding Lane and spread rapidly, damaging St. Paul's Cathedral and Charles 11's court in Whitehall. The Medieval city was overcrowded, and buildings made of wood and thatch burnt quickly. Many things got swept into the river during that time.
The Society of Thames Mudlarks	The Society was formed in 1976 by a group of specialists approved by the Museum of London and granted licences from the Port of London Authority. Membership is capped at 50 in London, and members can dig to a depth of 1.2m using hand tools. They have a special permit letting members search the North Bank of the River Thames when they wear or show their member's number.

Glossary of mudlarking terms	What does it mean?
Types of Tide	A Neap Tide is seven days after a Spring Tide, a period of moderate tides when the sun and moon are at right angles to each other. On a Spring Tide, the sun, moon and earth are all lined up, and the sun's tidal force works with the moon's tidal force. High tides are higher, and low tides are lower than average.
UK Treasure Act 1996 and Treasure	The UK Treasure Act 1996 defines Treasure and regulates how items should be dealt with. Under the Act, any object found in the UK that is at least 300 years old and contains a minimum amount of gold or silver or is of significant historical or archaeological interest, such as coins, is considered treasure. When treasure is found in the UK, the finder must report it to the local coroner within 14 days.
Upriver and downriver	Upriver is the direction of a river or stream towards its starting point inland. Downriver follows the direction of the river flowing down to the sea.
Waterman	A waterman is a river worker who takes passengers across and along city centre rivers and estuaries. Years ago, the watermen went down to the river using the staircases between the built-up waterfront buildings, especially in Wapping. Some staff who run the Uber Boats on the Thames are watermen – ask them when you next travel on the river.

Glossary of mudlarking terms	What does it mean?
Weil's disease	Weil's disease is spread by rat urine in the water. Infection is usually through cuts in the skin or through the eyes, mouth or nose. Flu-like symptoms include a temperature and aching in the muscles and joints, so seek medical advice if you feel unwell.
World Heritage Site – Tower of London foreshore	Area from Tower of London foreshore from the upstream side of Tower Bridge to the upstream side of the brow of Tower Pier where entry is forbidden. This area is labelled in black on the PLA river map.

Coins can be treasure

Mudlarking books and Magazines

Many books have been written about mudlarking, and there are some great blogs and Instagram, YouTube and Facebook accounts providing well-researched accounts of finds.

Mudlarking books and Magazines	Author and links
A Field Guide to Larking	Lara Maiklem
A Mudlark's Treasures – London in fragments	Ted Sandling
A-Z London Hidden Walks: Discover 20 routes in and around the city	Pete Smith
Beachcombing Magazine	A magazine dedicated to beachcombing, beach travel, coastal arts, and coastal living with mudlarking features. https://www.beachcombingmagazine.com/
Buckles 1250 – 1800 (including price guide)	Ross Whitehead
I never knew that about the River Thames	Christopher Winn
Logbook For A Mudlark: A lovely way to record all your finds	CarMez Publications
London Clay	Tom Chivers @thisisyogic
London The Biography	Peter Ackroyd
Mudlark – In Search of London's Past Along the River Thames	Lara Maiklem
Mudlark River Down The Thames with a Victorian Map	Simon Wilcox
Mudlark'd: Hidden histories from the River Thames	Malcolm Russell and Matthew Williams-Ellis
Mudlarking: A historical sourcebook	Heritage Hunter (author), Andrew Chapman (editor)
Mudlarking: Lost and Found on the River Thames	Lara Maiklem

Mudlarking books and Magazines	Author and links
Mudlarks: Treasures from the Thames	Jason Sandy
Rag and Bone: A Family History of What We've Thrown Away	Lisa Woollett
Thames Mudlarking: Searching for London's Lost Treasures	Jason Sandy, Nick Stevens
Thames Sacred River	Peter Ackroyd
The London Thames Path	David Fathers
The Mudlark's Log Book: A Place to Records and Track Your Finds	Rosalie Reeves
The River's Tale Archaeology on the Thames foreshore in Greater London	Nathalie Cohen and Eliott Wragg with Jon Cotton and Gustav Milne
Tokens and Tallies Through the Ages	Ted Fletcher
Treasure Hunting Magazine	https://www.treasurehunting.co.uk/

Tours and walks

These organisations run tours, taking people down to different parts of the foreshore – Thames Explorer Trust, Thames Discovery Programme, Thames Festival Trust, and Southwark Cathedral Walks (2023). I've listed what they do for each area. You can book a place online. You don't need a permit to join in, but only permit holders can keep finds. These are their descriptions.

Groups with Mudlark Tours

Groups with Mudlark Tours	What they do
Creekside Discovery Centre, Deptford	A charity with a nature park and creekside, working with schools, people and companies through river and wildflower walks and talks, sharing knowledge and know-how. Take a low tide walk in the Creek, safely looked after by expert guides. https://www.creeksidecentre.org.uk
Southwark Cathedral	Regular walks to the riverbank are led by Mike Webber, a community archaeologist, educator, and curator. https://cathedral.southwark.anglican.org/

Groups with Mudlark Tours	What they do
The Thames Discovery Programme (TDP)	TDP leads regular guided walks on the foreshore for adults and families with older children and teenagers. Walks focus on the history and heritage of the river and include structures and features exposed by the movement of sediment, which is monitored and archaeologically recorded by their Foreshore Recording and Observation Group (FROGs). Some surface-only artefact handling may be permitted on a TDP foreshore walk. All finds must be examined by the archaeologist. http://www.thamesdiscovery.org
The Thames Explorer Trust	This organisation runs guided public foreshore walks at Greenwich, Rotherhithe, Wapping, Limehouse and the Millennium Bridge. Money raised from these sessions supports the development and delivery of schools' programmes. https://thames-explorer.org.uk/
The Thames Festival Trust	This organisation runs Totally Thames, a month-long festival with walks, talks, and creative events. Their director says, 'Rivers run like arteries through the heart of our communities and are a source of inspiration, of joy and delight.' https://thamesfestivaltrust.org/

These are the areas they visit along the river with their descriptions. (2023)

Wapping Tour

The Thames Discovery Programme Wapping walk starts at the river stairs next to the Town of Ramsgate Pub in Wapping. You learn about the oldest operational police station in Britain, the history of the river police and the history of crime and punishment in this area.

Thames Explorer Trust Wapping walk starts at the River View Chinese restaurant at 1 New Crane Place, Wapping and goes down the steps to the foreshore.

Rotherhithe Tour

The Thames Discovery Programme (TDP) runs a foreshore walk on Rotherhithe Beach, describing the archaeology and history of the river. Surface-only artefact handling is permitted when attending a TDP foreshore walk, but all finds must be examined by the archaeologist on site, and significant artefacts must be recorded.

Thames Explorer Trust runs a two-hour Rotherhithe walk from the Brunel Museum, then down to the foreshore at Rotherhithe Beach.

Thames Festival Trust runs 'Once upon a time in Rotherhithe' from Bermondsey Tube Station, which ends at The Mayflower Pub. 400 years ago, the Pilgrims sailed from here when it was a small village. Buildings were built from a shipwreck, and there's a Church with masts for pillars and chairs carved from ships. See a Pirate's gibbet, The Watch House, which guards the graveyard, a memorial to Christopher Jones, Captain of the Mayflower, and another to Prince Lee Boo, a hero from the Spice Islands.

Putney Bridge Tour

The *Thames Discovery Programme* runs a Fulham Palace Walk on the north bank, which starts at the top of the river stairs in Bishops

Park, nearest to Putney Bridge. You learn about the wealth and power of the Bishops of London, seek out evidence of Iron Age activity on the shore and find out why a bridge was built here and what the first bridge was like. They also run walks on the south bank.

Southbank Tour
The Thames Discovery Programme Bankside foreshore walk starts at the top of the river stairs next to the Founders Arms Pub. You learn about how an area of marshes and islands became the entertainment centre of Tudor London, seek out evidence of 19th century industry and find out about public transport on the Thames in days gone by.

The Thames Festival Trust tour along the North Bank explores the foreshore from Millennium Bridge to Southwark Bridge. During the tour, you can only take photographs, knowledge and memories, but not the artefacts themselves.

Southwark Cathedral Walk goes west along Bankside, where the foreshore walk begins. You will be on the foreshore for 1.5 – 2 hours. Only those with a special permit issued by the Port of London Authority (PLA) can take objects found on the foreshore.

North Bank City Tours
Queenhithe Dock is a protected Scheduled Ancient Monument, and permit holders can only search on the shoreline, not in the dock area.

The Thames Explorer Trust Millennium Bridge tour starts at the Millennium Bridge on the North Bank and explores the foreshore from the bridge to Queenhithe Dock. You may find smoking pipes, drainpipes, pottery, bones, Tudor roof tiles and bricks, and even pieces of Roman pottery.

Southwark Cathedral runs a guided walk with an archaeologist. The walk starts at Southwark Cathedral and goes over London Bridge to the City of London, where the foreshore walk begins. You will be on the foreshore for 1.5 – 2 hours. Only those with a special permit issued by the Port of London Authority (PLA) can take objects found on the foreshore.

Thames Festival Trust Millennium Bridge tour starts at the Millennium Bridge on the North Bank and explores the foreshore from the bridge to Queenhithe Dock. You may find smoking pipes, drainpipes, pottery, bones, Tudor roof tiles and bricks, and even pieces of Roman pottery.

Greenwich Tour
The Thames Discovery Programme Greenwich walk

This organisation runs walks taking people with and without a licence, and this walk starts at the Old Royal Naval College with easy access to the foreshore. You learn about Henry VIII's favourite palace in Greenwich and how it became a retirement home for naval sailors and then a college for training naval officers. You'll find out about the care of people experiencing poverty in nearby almshouses and see the structures used to maintain boats and ships.

My favourite riverside walks
Six walks beside the river that I really enjoy, with notes on the history of the area, suggestions for river access and possible finds if you are mudlarking.

1. Wapping Walk – North Bank – Tower Bridge to The Prospect of Whitby Pub
2. Rotherhithe Walk – South Bank – Tower Bridge to Rotherhithe Beach

3. Putney Bridge Walk – Putney Bridge to Hammersmith Bridge, South Bank returning North Bank
4. South Bank Walk – London Bridge to Westminster Bridge
5. City of London Walk – Cannon Street Station to Blackfriars Bridge
6. Greenwich Walk – Greenwich Pier from east to west, Deptford and part of the Isle of Dogs

Wapping Walk

Tower Bridge to The Prospect of Whitby Pub

This is a fascinating walk along the North Bank of the Thames Path into an old part of the east London docklands. You get a feel for this busy trading area when you travel along the cobbled streets, down narrow alleyways onto the foreshore and visit some lovely old pubs.

John Stow, a 16th century historian, described Wapping as a 'continual street, or a filthy strait passage, with alleys of small tenements or cottages, built, inhabited by sailors and victuallers, who supplied food, beverages and other provisions for the crew of a vessel at sea.'

A 1746 map of London shows an area busy with taverns, brothels, wharves, warehouses and narrow alleyways that led down to the foreshore for journeys across the river in an area that bustled with activity and river travel. Some stairs with access to this part of the river have disappeared, and some have changed their names.

The major industry in Wapping was shipbuilding, but it became part of a busy port of London with a large complex of docks. Bombing by the German Luftwaffe during the Second World War had a devastating effect on the warehouses, factories and docks in the Wapping area, and as you walk on the cobbles of Wapping High Street, notice how new, modern buildings have been built next to the old, converted warehouses.

By the 1970s, the area changed radically as the riverside docks closed. Bigger ships carried cargoes loaded in containers, and these ships needed to dock further out to sea in container ports like Tilbury. Local people were rehoused from the bombed-out area and moved to new towns like Harlow in Essex. By the 1990s, Wapping was being developed into trendy flats in the converted warehouses with amazing views over the Thames and easy access for people working in the skyscrapers of Canary Wharf or the city. You'll find on this route that access to the river walk is sometimes restricted.

Alderman Stairs

Start

Arrive on the riverside in front of the Tower of London by the Uber Boat at Tower Millennium Pier, Tower Hill tube station or use the many buses. The walk takes you east along the Thames Path beside the river until you reach the famous Pelican Stairs next to The Prospect of Whitby Pub.

Some of the alleys down to the river used by the wherrymen have fallen into disrepair and are closed, but there are several sets of stairs with variable ease of access to the foreshore at low tide through the old alleyways.

1. Walk along the cobbled Tower Wharf promenade in front of the Tower of London, past Traitors' Gate, which was the Medieval prison entrance to the Tower with steps leading down to the river behind locked gates. Many famous people, including Queen Anne Boleyn and Sir Thomas More, were brought here by river to be imprisoned in the Tower. This foreshore is now a protected area with no access.
2. Follow the Thames Path under Tower Bridge, then past Tower Hotel, a large, imposing building. Cross over the footbridge in front of St Katharine Docks and wind your way along St Katharine's Way, where you can pop into Devon House, a modern building built on the site of a bomb-damaged warehouse, with a coffee shop and a large outside patio overlooking the Thames, and great views and photo-opportunities towards Tower Bridge and The Shard.
3. Carry on along St Katharine's Way to Alderman Stairs, the first set of stairs you pass that watermen used to get to the river. Go down the alley and climb down stone stairs to a stone slipway. The iron gates were open when we tested, but the steps are slippery when the tide goes out. There are great views up and down the river and over to Butlers Wharf.
4. Return to walk east along the Thames Path beside the river in front of Tower Bridge Wharf, which was once a six-storey warehouse that stored cargo, including wine and tea. You can choose either to walk along Wapping High Street or the riverwalk with more spectacular views. Pass Hermitage Riverside Memorial Gardens with a sculpture of a dove, a symbol of hope, in memory of the East London civilians killed or injured in the Second World War.
5. Hermitage Stairs are at the east end of the gardens and in poor condition, with a huge jump down the riverbed. Hermitage Community Moorings have berths with historic vessels, and on open days, you can talk to the residents and discover what it's like to live on board.

Wapping Old Stairs

6. Walk along Wapping High Street, past Pier Head, with handsome houses built in 1811 for officials of the London Dock Company and with private access to the river for residents only. You come to Wapping Old Stairs East, west of the Town Of Ramsgate Pub. The pub is a 16th century ale house, one of the thirty-six that once served Wapping High Street. It takes its name from the fishermen of Ramsgate who landed their catch at Wapping Old Stairs. The pub's cellars were where convicted criminals were kept before they were hanged, and later on, the cellars held convicts before they were transported by ship to Australia. The stone stairs beside the pub have a wall rail and lead down to a jetty and the sandy, shingly foreshore, but they can be slippery with green algae.
7. Return and walk along Wapping High Street, which was built in the 1500s to link the riverside quays with the City of London. In the 16th century, it was described as a 'filthy passage, with alleys of small tenements and cottages ... whose

many inhabitants were victuallers who supplied sailors with maritime equipment and just as importantly cheap alcohol and women'.

8. Walk along the waterfront along Waterside Gardens and past Wapping New Stairs with an iron gate that opens down stone stairs leading to a ladder with challenging access to the foreshore, which runs to the east. Several mudlarks were down on the shingle there as we passed.

9. Back on Wapping High Street, walk east, past the Metropolitan Marine Policing Unit. The sides of this unusual 1970s building are decorated with unusual shapes. The next alleyway to the shore is blocked with a Danger sign, but take a look inside the Captain Kidd Pub with a terrace that overlooks the river, one of the largest on this stretch of the Thames. Go past the pub and down an alley to King Henry Steps with stone steps, where people access the river using a wobbly ladder. We did not test this as it looked unsafe. This beach may be the site of Execution Dock, where prisoners were hung on the foreshore. The bodies were left hanging here until three tides had washed over them to act as a warning to other pirates or smugglers.

10. Back along Wapping High Street and past King Henry's Wharves and Gun Wharves, named because this was where Henry VIII built a foundry to make cannons for his navy. On to Wapping Rail Station, where stairs to the west of the station have a locked gate and no access. Before the road curves to the left, you come to New Crane Stairs, which go down to the river beside River View Chinese Restaurant. These stone steps have a small jump down to the shingle, giving easy access to a long piece of interesting foreshore. Thames Explorer Trust uses these stairs for their mudlarking event In the Footsteps of Mudlarks. You can walk east along this foreshore to Pelican Stairs and the Prospect of Whitby Pub. At one section, you have to

scramble over and under large wooden posts supporting a pier at low tide.

11. Back to Wapping High Street and turn right onto Wapping Wall, then carry along until you reach Pelican Stairs to the west side of The Prospect of Whitby Pub, which opened in 1520. Stone stairs lead down to wooden ones and can be slippery. The pub has a hangman's rope noose dangling outside the riverside windows to remind us of the pirates and baddies hanged in the area in the 18th century. Climb down to the foreshore onto Wapping Beach, with a wide, shingly foreshore at low tide with lots of space for mudlarking. Whistler and Turner painted some of their most famous riverside scenes from here, and it was a regular drinking place for Charles Dickens and Samuel Pepys.

12. End the walk here and catch the D3 bus back into the City, or walk to Wapping Station or head on east to Canary Wharf Pier, where you can catch the Uber Boat back to the City.

Prospect of Whitby

Did you know? Fun facts about Wapping

1. Garnet Street in Wapping, despite its name, has nothing to do with semi-precious stones. The street was called New Gravel Lane, the route for carrying sand and gravel inland from the riverside. The name was changed to honour Thomas Garnett, an ordained priest suspected of involvement in the Gunpowder Plot.
2. The Thames River Police Museum on Wapping High Street is inside the Metropolitan Police's Marine Police Unit, housed in an old carpenter's workshop and the headquarters of the river police. Its exhibits show the history of the world's first police force from when it started in 1798 to the present day. The museum is not open to the public, but you can make an appointment to visit and discover the fascinating stories of this part of the Thames.
3. The Prospect of Whitby Pub is near Execution Dock, where, in the 17th century, pirates were hanged. Judge Jeffreys was called the Hanging Judge as he sentenced nearly seven hundred people to be punished and was known to dine at the pub so that he could watch the hangings over a spot of lunch. I hope he enjoyed his pies.
4. The pirate, Captain Kidd, who gave his name to the pub, was hanged at Execution Dock in 1701. He was supposed to have given Robert Louis Stevenson ideas for his characters in his novel Treasure Island.

Rotherhithe Walk
London Bridge to Rotherhithe Beach

A historic walk from the South Bank from Tower Bridge to Rotherhithe Beach along the Thames Path with great photographic views when you look back to The Shard, Tower Bridge and the skyscrapers of the City. This area was a bustling trading area, with plenty of ships and barges moored along the river, ships were taken apart when they were no longer needed, and coal was delivered to the power stations and homes along this part of the river. Rotherhithe is famous as it's where the Pilgrim Fathers departed for America in 1620, and it's worth popping into the Mayflower Pub and visiting St. Mary's Church to catch up on the history.

If you look over to the east of the north bank of the Thames you'll see beaches at Tower Bridge and in front of Custom House. Entry to both these beaches is prohibited – check the PLA map for restrictions.

Custom House Beach

Start

1. Start on the South Bank of Tower Bridge, joining part of the Thames Path into Butler's Wharf, completed in 1871. Enter Horselydown, a historic London area south of the river by Tower Bridge. Horselydown Old Stairs (also spelt Horsleydown) are on the left and run along a small passageway to a stony beach. The stairs have a handrail but can be slippery. This area was called London's Larder in the 19th century as so many goods were unloaded here. In the 16th century, Flemish refugees arrived with beer-making skills and opened many riverfront breweries and pubs along the water from London Bridge to Horselydown. It's a narrow beach with large, uneven stones to scramble over.
2. Walk along Shad Thames, a dark street with overhanging warehouses, then turn left down Maggie Blake's Cause to walk along the riverfront. Look up above the restaurants and see the enormous warehouses that have been turned into sought-after apartments. There's a small white building between two Butler's Wharf buildings, once a banana warehouse, it opened in 1989 as Sir Terence Conran's Design Museum, which closed in 2016 and moved to Kensington.
3. Cross the stainless steel footbridge at the entrance to St. Saviour's Dock. Here, the bodies of the captured and hanged pirates went on display. Yuk. Walk past New Concordia Wharf and Jacob's Island Pier then the Thames Path goes under the building on the river frontage.
4. You need to weave along this part of the riverbank as it twists around old and new buildings. Take the narrow ramped path down to Mill Street, along Bermondsey Wall West, turn right down East Lane, then left into Chambers Street, and left into Loftie Street, and then along the road as it bends to the right.

Take the next left to walk through Fountain Green Square to return to the riverside and the Thames Path. Whew!

5. Continue along the Thames – the walk changes directions with new building works. Here, Tideway is creating the huge Super Sewer under the river, and views will change when it is completed.
6. Bermondsey Beach has concrete steps down to the foreshore by Bermondsey Wall. More steps by Cherry Garden Pier descend to the foreshore, with handrails to a beach area. At low tide, you can walk westwards to Hidden Beach, a rather shingly area beneath Tideway. Samuel Pepys recorded in his diaries visiting Cherry Gardens to buy cherries for his wife, and here J.M.W. Turner saw HMS Temeraire being towed to be broken down, which inspired his painting, The Fighting Temeraire.
7. After Cherry Garden Pier, go back to the road and turn left along Bermondsey Wall East with statues of the Salters, a doctor and his wife, who famously improved the lives of people in the slums of Bermondsey. Rotherhithe Stairs are on the west side of the historic Angel Pub at the end of the road, with access to the river and the wide Bermondsey Beach, a popular site for mudlarks and Thames beach tours.
8. King's Stairs are modern stairs to the west of the tall, thin house called The Leaning Tower of Rotherhithe. The gate at the top was open when checked but the stairs were slippery. The house was the main office of a barge company where their lightermen, who operated on the Thames, pulled up to get their wages. Rotherhithe Stairs and the King's Stairs were used by the original mudlarks who scavenged the riverbank at low tide, finding coal, discarded iron, copper nails, lost tools, old bones, and sometimes lifting cargo from the many barges moored there. Across the river, you can see Execution Dock, where pirates were executed by hanging.

Mayflower Pub

9. Carry along the Thames Path and turn left on Elephant Lane onto Rotherhithe Street. St. Mary's Church is the burial place for four of The Mayflower's owners, including Christopher Jones, who captained the ship to the New World. Church Steps are on the west side of The Mayflower Pub on Rotherhithe Street but are very steep and have a gate at the top by the pub, which may be locked. If open, clamber with care down through wooden pillars to get to the beach. Watch the tide, as this is a pinch point. These steps could be an

important escape route from the beach if the tide comes in quickly.
10. Walk along the Thames Path through a small garden area to the river above Rotherhithe Beach, a great area for mudlarking with a wide beach which you can visit after other Thames beaches are covered in river water. Rotherhithe Beach steps are easy stone steps leading down to the wide, sandy foreshore by a large moored boat. Rotherhithe was a shipbuilding and trading area, and you'll find plenty of ironware, copper nails and even trade beads on the foreshore. I've met mudlarks who found musket and cannon balls among the shingle.
11. At low tide, you can mudlark back to Bermondsey Beach, return to Rotherhithe station, or get the bus back into the centre.

Did you know? Fun facts about Rotherhithe

1. The Fighting Temeraire painting, in the National Gallery, was painted by Joseph Mallord William Turner in 1839. It shows the final sad journey of the old warship, The Temeraire, being towed by a steam tug along the River Thames to the breakers yard in Rotherhithe, where it was scrapped and broken down. The Temeraire was one of the largest warships that took part in the Battle of Trafalgar, and its last voyage took on a symbolic meaning as the age of sail gave way to the age of steam. Perhaps bits of the ship can be found on the foreshore today.
2. On May 6th 1621, the Mayflower ship was brought back to Rotherhithe on its final voyage and left to deteriorate in the river beside the Shippe Tavern. Stories tell that the ship's timbers were used to rebuild the inn, which was renamed The Mayflower in 1957 in honour of the Pilgrim's ship. It's the only pub in Britain licenced to sell British and American postage stamps.

Putney Bridge Walk
Circular by Hammersmith Bridge on the South Bank and back on the North Bank

This circular river walk takes about two hours if you don't linger on the foreshore, and when I've taken visitors new to London around this loop along the leafy pathways, some think we are walking in the countryside. There's evidence that people have lived and travelled along this part of the river since Neolithic times as they left behind their flint tools made into axes, arrowheads, adzes and scrapers used for hunting, fishing, preparing food, and maybe fighting off intruders. You can find examples in the Collections of The British Museum and the Museum of London. At very low tides on this walk, on the north foreshore by Fulham Palace, you might see the early Medieval fish traps dated to AD 410-640, prehistoric peat beds and wooden posts where Anglo-Saxon travellers tied up their boats. The Thames had an important river crossing here, an area used by the Romans who had settlements nearby.

Years ago, in Wandsworth, Putney, and Fulham, there were many fisheries where they caught freshwater fish such as smelt, salmon, and eels. Some of the fish were bought and sold at Billingsgate fish market, a journey east along the river to the City.

When Putney Bridge opened in 1729 on the site of the Putney Ferry, it was the first new permanent bridge after London Bridge on the 29-mile stretch of the river between Kingston and London Bridge. The wooden bridge deteriorated and was replaced in 1886 with the new Putney Bridge, which Sir Joseph Bazalgette designed. He was famous for creating the sewerage system for central London, which cleaned up the river after The Great Stink. He also designed Hammersmith Bridge, a beautiful suspension bridge crossing from Barnes to Hammersmith. It's only open to pedestrians and cyclists but not road traffic as it's undergoing extensive repairs.

Thames Bridge

Start

1. Start on the east side of Putney Bridge on the south side of the river, and go down the stone steps to the shingle on the foreshore. Wander east towards Wandsworth and the houseboat homes moored near Wandsworth Riverside Quarter Pier. Return along the foreshore to Putney, where there's easy access up the slipway to Brewhouse Lane.
2. Otherwise, carry along the foreshore under Putney Bridge and climb up the slipway on the west side of Putney Bridge beside the Tideway platform, recently built on top of the Super Sewer. Have a look at the ventilation column on top of the site and read the poem chiselled into the side of the stone using letters from the salvaged Doves Press Font. See details at the end.
3. Head west along the Thames Path past Putney Pier, where the Uber Boat leaves to travel into the City and onto Greenwich. Walk past the boat yards and the area where the Oxford and Cambridge Boat Race starts. The river here gets busy with rowers and pleasure cruises, and there are always plenty of geese, swans and cormorants paddling on the shoreline looking for food in the water.

4. Head straight along the Thames Path with Leader's Gardens on your left, busy with families with small children and a small café which serves cakes and sandwiches, then cross the bridge over Beverly Brook. You're in the wooded area of the path, but watch out for the many runners and bikes that speed along.
5. Walk beside the river, past the boundary of the London Wetland Centre on your left. The site is formed of four disused Victorian reservoirs tucked into a loop in the Thames, and you may see flocks of wild birds flying over to visit the lakes.
6. On this part of the Thames Path, there are several sets of steps on the righthand grassy bank leading to the foreshore, but many are steep, with no handrail, so take care. Keep walking west past the very grand Harrods Furniture Depository built in 1894 with the famous department store's signature orangey-pink brickwork. In those days, the five-storey warehouse was offered to customers as a storage space for their furniture while they were abroad. It's now been converted into townhouses and apartments with views over the river. The stairs to the west of the Harrods Furniture Depository have a handrail down to the river.

Hammersmith Bridge

7. Walk on to Hammersmith Bridge, one of the world's oldest suspension bridges, which is currently being repaired. If you carry on along the footpath beyond the Bridge, heading west to Barnes, you can climb steps down to the foreshore and discover the famous Wet Wipe Island, a rather revolting sight of grey, ragged detritus from the sewers.
8. Turn right to cross over Hammersmith Bridge to the North Bank, which is where Doves Type was thrown into the water – an extremely sought-after find by mudlarks. There are tricky access points in the river wall to descend the ramps to the foreshore. Walk east to Putney and head along the Thames Path past Riverside Studios, where you can stop for a drink or a snack. Ladders attached to the riverbank wall give access to a very muddy foreshore, but these haven't been tested, and there is a slipway with a planted garden.
9. The walk on the North Bank takes you past the famous River Café, probably one of the best restaurants in London and worth booking for a meal. Pop in for a peek and admire their stylish flower arrangements and huge pizza oven. Carry on by the river and enjoy the amazing views over the water to The Wetlands. Eventually, your walk is diverted to Stevenage Road, around Craven Cottage, the Fulham Football Stadium, which one day, hopefully, will open its riverwalk to the public.
10. Turn right to go back by the river into part of Fulham Palace grounds. The Palace was once the Tudor home of the Bishops of London, so who knows what they dropped in the river as they made their journey to and fro from the City of London? Fulham Palace is open to the public and has a well-tended walled garden and greenhouse, which are free to enter. It's really worth a detour to visit. There is a café in Bishop's Park and Fulham Palace. Check the opening times.
11. Midway along the walk in Bishop's Park, there are concrete steps down to a thin strip of foreshore, which can be quite muddy.

12. Further along the path, you come to Bishop's Steps or Ferry Steps near Putney Bridge, giving access to the riverbank. Climb over the Victorian rails down the concrete steps, which can be muddy and slippery, onto the shingly foreshore. Turn east and wander under Putney Bridge and below the green, heavy lattice girders of Fulham Railway Bridge. Here, the foreshore is wide, and at low tide, you have plenty of time to watch rowers on the river and mudlark. Be aware that the incoming tide can be fast.
13. Return west to Putney Bridge and travel back by tube, bus, rail or, my favourite, the Uber Boat from Putney Pier, which glides east towards the City past glorious river views.

Doves font

Did you know? Fun facts about Putney and Hammersmith

1. Doves Type – The absolute top of my Mudlark Wishlist would be to find a piece of Doves Press font with its famous story of being thrown off Hammersmith Bridge over 100 years ago after a disagreement between the owners of Doves Press publishing company. Doves Roman was regarded as one of the most beautiful fonts of all time, but the partnership between Mr Walker and Mr Cobden-Sanderson broke down. On 21 March 1913, Mr Cobden-Sanderson threw pieces of the type into the Thames off Hammersmith Bridge. He made an estimated 170 trips by foot and tipped the type, weighing over a ton, into the Thames. Now for the good news. In November 2014, the Port of London Authority's diving team, directed by the designer Robert Green, salvaged 151 pieces of the drowned typeface from the Thames, and these salvaged pieces helped Green to recreate the typeface. And the story goes on. The Doves Type was commissioned as the font for lettering Tideway's architectural objects, such as walls, railings, paving, and ventilation columns, which you can see all along the river, like the one near Putney Pier.
2. Poet Dorothea Smartt was commissioned to write poems for nine ventilation columns at the Thames Tideway Tunnel sites. You can get close to them on your river walks. All of Smartt's poems are linked to London's 'Lost Rivers', and the poems had to be short, about 150 characters, so they would fit along the columns and be easily read.
3. Wet Wipe Island Hammersmith on the south side of the river at Hammersmith has piles of soggy, grey Wet Wipes piled on the foreshore when sewage overflow gets dumped. On this bend in the river, the water moves slowly, and Wet Wipes, sanitary products, and other raggy stuff twist around discarded branches on the foreshore. Thames21 has been tracking Wet Wipes on the Thames with their

Big Wet Wipe Counts since 2017, and in 2023, I joined a jolly group of Thames21 volunteers to carry out a scientific survey, collecting and counting Wet Wipes on this part of the riverbank. This River Action Group, with scientists, has collected more than 137,000 wipes over 94 clean-up events across London. Wet Wipes cause 75% of drain blockages, and they account for the biggest cause of fatbergs. Thames21 have asked for the sale of Wet Wipes to be controlled and for fewer sewage overflows to be allowed into the river.

Wet Wipes

South Bank Walk
From London Bridge to The London Eye

Years ago, the south bank of the river was bustling with people crossing over on business, visiting the theatres and bear and cock fighting, as well as brothels, inns and ale houses. Bankside became London's entertainment centre, licenced by the Bishops of Winchester, and in the 19th century, there was a lot of industry, with several power stations were built here. The South Bank in central London is once again a popular destination for tourists and locals, with access points down to the foreshore from the London Eye to Tower Bridge.

The area has a long sandy beach at low tide, and with luck, below Gabriels Wharf, the talented sand sculptor may be at work, digging and creating fantastic shapes out of sand on the beach. Talk to him and take his Instagram link – he has some great tales to tell.

Today, modern rubbish like food packaging and drinks cartons often litter the foreshore, but several volunteer groups carry out rubbish collections and clear up the riverbank.

OXO Tower

Start

1. Start your walk from London Bridge City Pier, where you can arrive by Uber Boat, or make your way by tube, train or bus to London Bridge and head west along the South Bank

with views of the giant City skyscrapers on the North Bank. On the North Bank, you can see Horizon 22, with London's highest free viewing platform and Sky Garden with great river views from the 35th floor.
2. Walk under London Bridge onto Montague Close and pass The Mudlark Pub, named after the 18th century mudlarks who scavenged nearby. Southwark Cathedral has mudlarking walks, talks and London's first permanent Mudlarking Exhibition with a monthly star find from the foreshore and a different guest display every three months. One display had pilgrim badges found on the riverbank near the Cathedral.
3. There is no access to the river until you get past Southwark Bridge. It's a busy walk along this historic part of Bankside, past The Golden Hinde, The Clink Prison Museum, The Premier Inn, where visiting mudlarks stay for early morning foraging, and The Anchor Pub Bankside.
4. Go under Southwark Bridge and see river steps on the west side with a gate. Sometimes, this gate is locked, but if not, push it open and descend the stone steps, which can be slimy with algae. The foreshore runs east and west of the stairs.
5. Carry on along the Bankside path and look left down Bear Gardens Street, which led to the bear baiting area in Shakespeare's time. An old Ferryman's Seat has been set in the east wall that Bankside watermen used.
6. Stone stairs in front of The Globe Theatre beside Bankside Pier lead down to the river, but there are slimy bits at the bottom and no handrail down to Bankside Beach. Chains hang down from river walls to help balance, but there's a steep drop onto the shoreline.
7. The stone stairs in front of Tate Modern are well maintained, with easy access to a sandy beach through a gate but no handrail. If time allows, visit the 6th floor of Tate Modern, with great views over the Thames to St. Paul's Cathedral

and the Millenium Bridge. The Tate's highest platform at the top of the Blavatnik Building has reopened, and renamed Level 10. Both are free to visit.
8. Carry along Bankside to stone stairs in front of The Founder's Arms Pub, which are in good condition with no handrail. The gate on the path opens for access down to the sandy foreshore.

Bankside Stairs

9. Cross under Blackfriars' Railway Station Bridge and to the east of Blackfriars Bridge, where the stone stairs had a locked metal gate and no access when tested.
10. Cross Blackfriars Bridge, down steps in front of the Doggett's Coat and Badge Pub, which has a famous annual river rowing

race. There are stone stairs down to the river in reasonably good condition but slippery at the bottom with rails down, but the gate is sometimes locked.

11. Walk along the Thames Path to the OXO Tower overlooking Thames Beach. There is a free public viewing on the 8th floor of the OXO Tower, in between the brasserie and the restaurant, with glorious views over the river, St. Paul's, and the City. The OXO Tower has the best metal stairs down to the river on the west side of the OXO building, with sturdy handrails to a sandy beach and access to a long stretch of riverbank.

12. Stone stairs below Gabriel's Wharf give easy access with handrails down to the sandy beach, where you may see the sand sculptor. Gabriel's Wharf is an interesting small shopping and dining area on the South Bank riverfront.

13. Stone stairs in front of The National Theatre have a gate leading down to another sandy area of the foreshore. As you walk along The Queen's Walk, pause at the Southbank Skate space with walls decorated with colourful graffiti and be amazed by the skateboarders showing off their tricks and jumps.

14. Stairs on both sides of Festival Pier lead down to another sandy area of the foreshore, but locked metal gates prevent easy access. There's a blue sign saying 'Reclaim the Beach from 1934 and revived in 2017', telling us that the children of London should have 'free access to the beach forever' to the beach below. This sign was erected in the hope that the beach would have more public use at low tide.

15. Carry on along the river, heading west. If you want another sky-high view over London, buy a ticket for The London Eye, Europe's tallest cantilevered observation wheel and the UK's most popular tourist attraction. The Uber Boat leaves from Westminster Pier to take trips up and down the river.

Did you know? Fun facts about London Bridge to Westminster Bridge

1. Where did The OXO Tower get its name from? In the 19th century, the building was a power station and then purchased for cold storage by the Liebig Extract of Meat Company, which made OXO Beef Stock Cubes. The architect, Albert Moore, incorporated the letters OXO into the windows on the tower to get around a ban on skyline advertising, and they still glow with red lights at night. OXO Tower Wharf has studios for designer-makers, and you can watch them at work and order unique designs of fine art, textiles, jewellery and ceramics.

Shakespeare's Globe Theatre

2. Shakespeare's Globe was built as close to the site of the Old Globe Theatre as possible and completed in 1997. The actor and director Sam Wanamaker founded the theatre, which is a realistic true-to-history reconstruction of The Globe, an Elizabethan playhouse first built in 1599 for which William

Shakespeare wrote his plays. Like the original theatre, the stage projects into a large circular yard surrounded by three tiers of raked seating. The only covered parts of the theatre are the stage and the seating areas, so if it's raining, wear wet weather clothing if you are going to a play. There are daily behind-the-scenes tours.
3. The Tate Modern Art Gallery is housed in the former Bankside Power Station, designed by the same architect as Battersea Power Station. Bankside closed in 1981 and was at risk of demolition but was converted into London's free National Museum of Modern and Contemporary Art and opened in May 2000. In 1889, Henry Tate, a successful sugar refiner, provided funding for the first Tate Gallery and gave his name to the other museums. See more about him in the section on Sugar.

City of London Walk
Cannon Street Station to Trig Lane Stairs North Bank

Queenhithe Dock is a protected Scheduled Ancient Monument, and permit holders can only search on the shoreline, not in the dock area. This is an 'eyes only' area for mudlarks with no digging or scraping.

This is a short walk along the foreshore in parts of Londinium, the provincial capital of Roman Britain, which the Romans established in the first century AD. On the foreshore you can slowly crunch over history and examine the stones and shingle that may hide historical stuff that was thrown away and lost in this busy trading area. Imagine the changes from the Roman trading settlement to the glittering skyscrapers that now dominate the City's modern skyline.

Check out the changes on John Rocque's 18th century map of London. See the huge numbers of ships and barges moored on the river then and realise the trade and passage of people from long ago.

Above the river, walk along the North Bank and visit The Queenhithe Mosaic on the Thames Path, which shows the history of the area and includes mudlarks' foreshore finds like Roman pots and pilgrim badges. The artwork was commissioned by the City of London, 4C Hotel Group footed the bill and the mosaic was inspired by actual archaeological objects and discarded fragments from the Thames foreshore. One funny section of the mosaic shows there was a place of easement, meaning toilets, at Queenhithe, a facility that you won't find nearby today.

Down on the foreshore, take time to gaze around at famous London tourist sights as you overlook The Shard and famous London bridges. Look west towards Shakespeare's Globe, The Millenium Bridge, and over the river to the tall chimneys of Tate Modern. To the east, round the corner is the famous Tower Bridge which opens to let tall ships enter this part of the Thames. Imagine the changes in the landscape since the Romans left Londinium in AD 410.

At night, the buildings and bridges shimmer with different coloured lights, and you'll see the nightlarks searching the foreshore, wearing head torches as they move slowly along the shingle. Just for fun, call in at the Samuel Pepys Pub in nearby Stew Lane and glance down from the riverfront balcony at fellow mudlarks as they search the riverbank below. And no, the street didn't get its name from meat stew. From the 12th to the 17th century the Bishops rented out the brothels, known as 'stews' on their land, and the stews were licensed and regulated by the government 'to prevent any debauchery'.

My Walk – A North Bank walk from Cannon Street Station to Trig Lane Stairs

Start

1. Turn left out of Cannon Street tube, cross over Upper Thames Street, then walk to the end of Cousin Lane towards the river

where stone stairs lead down to the foreshore next to The Banker pub. There's a handrail on part of the stairway, the bottom steps can be slippery, and there's a jump down onto the foreshore. This part of the beach is for visual inspection only. Even turning over a stone to look underneath is off-limits. If you have a licence and see something on the surface, you can pick it up to have a look. Metal detectors, trowels and spades are forbidden.

2. If you turn east along the beach, you scramble over uneven, large stones under Cannon Street Railway Bridge, so take care. Here, you'll find plenty of bricks, old tiles, and lots of animal bones. This area is very popular with tours, mudlarks and members of the Society of Mudlarks, who have permission to dig holes and use metal detectors. They usually show a plaque with a number near where they dig, or wear an identity number on their back. If they are working in the area, ask their permission to sort through the pile of discarded earth. This is how I found two nit combs.

3. Climb over tricky concrete slabs onto the area below Hanseatic Walk. There is a ladder quite firmly attached to the river wall for foreshore access from above or below. At low tide this beach leads to a shingle area, and at really low tide, you can walk further along. Take care as the tide comes in quickly.

4. Retrace your steps and walk west under Cannon Street Railway Bridge to the large barge moored at Walbrook Wharf and carry on along the foreshore, where the now-hidden Walbrook River flowed into the Thames. The river was important in Roman London, and excavations along the buried river uncovered large amounts of Roman archaeology.

5. Walk along the rough foreshore until you approach four large arches. Low tide exposes the slippery concrete floor below the arches, where you can make your way carefully across to Queenhithe Beach. Take care with this part. Ask others

to show you dangerous places where you could get caught by incoming tides as the water travels fast in this part of the river.

Roman pot

6. Queenhithe was the Roman and Medieval quay and dock. Queenhithe Dock is now a Scheduled Ancient Monument, and you are not allowed to pick anything up at the top part of this area below The Westin London City Hotel. There was a harbour and markets in Queenhithe from AD 889, and through the later Medieval period, fish, grain, salt and timber were traded from here. This was where Charles II landed to survey the damage caused by the Great Fire Of London in 1666. I've found burnt pieces of tile nearby and imagined they were left over from those times.
7. Take time to watch the river life here, which is busy with tourists, Uber boats, and speed boats that travel east towards Canary Wharf for a fast thrill. The working river traffic, such

as the Police and Coastguard boats, frequently patrol this waterway.

8. Walk onto the wider beach below Paul's Walk with access from the famous Trig Lane Stairs by the north side of the Millennium Bridge. There's a sandy patch up by the river wall where people sit and chat, and an escape ladder is attached to the river wall. Scrunch your way along the gravelly, chalky shingle and be amazed as you walk over so many pipe stems, oyster shells, animal bones, red and yellow bricks, red roof tiles, and lumps of chalk.

Millenium Bridge

9. Enjoy watching the tourists clattering over the Millenium Bridge before you make your exit up Trig Lane Stairs. The lower half of the stairs has no handrail, so you need a good balance, and the steps are steep. Paul's Walk is part of the Thames Path at the top of the stairs. Look up at St. Paul's Cathedral, which is well worth a visit if you want a river view from the Dome with 528 steps to the top. Or join the many people crossing the Millenium Bridge over the river to Tate Modern and The Globe Theatre.

Pubs on the City of London Walk
The Westin, London City Hotel makes a great all-you-can-eat breakfast after a morning mudlark.

The Samuel Pepys Pub overlooks the river foreshore from its balcony.

Did you know? Fun facts about the City of London Walk
Lost London river

The Walbrook, one of London's lost rivers, once cut the City in half from Finsbury Circus to Cannon Street station. Archaeologists think the river may have been a boundary, industrial zone, or religious site and rare metal artefacts found in the waterlogged ground tell the story of the working lives of Roman Londoners. The Museum of London (closed 2023) has one of the largest collections of Roman tools in Europe, the majority of them coming from around the area of the Walbrook River.

The Millenium Bridge
The Bridge opened to the public in 2000 and links St. Paul's Cathedral on the Thames North Bank to Tate Modern and Shakespeare's Globe on the South Bank. The bridge was designed to resemble a blade of light across the River Thames, but on its opening day, around 90,000 people crossed, the bridge swayed and made some people feel sick. It got the nickname The Wobbly Bridge and had to be closed for two years to fix by putting dampers underneath. From the foreshore, mudlarks can look up and see the underside of the Bridge and spot the fixings used to stop the wobble.

The Queenhithe Mosaic
You can learn a lot from this colourful mosaic about the story of this part of the foreshore. The 30-metre-long mosaic runs along the Thames Path next to Queenhithe, showing 2,000 years of Thames history, starting with the Romans, moving to the Saxons when Queenhithe was called Ethelred's Hythe and goods were sold from

boats moored nearby. In the 12th century, the name changed to Queenhithe, and Queen Matilda was granted import taxes here. It's probably the only surviving Anglo-Saxon dock left in the world.

The mosaic shows archaeological discarded fragments picked up from the Thames foreshore. The mosaic was completed in 2014 and finishes with modern scenes of The Blitz and construction of the Millennium Bridge.

Oyster Cards

I love the story that holey oyster shells were traded for river crossings and gave their name to the London Oyster Card, although sadly, it was just an April Fool's joke.

Andrew McCrum, who invented the name Oyster Card writes -

'Oyster Card was conceived because of the metaphorical implications of security and value in the hard bivalve shell and the concealed pearl. Its associations with London through Thames Estuary oyster beds and the relevance of the popular saying 'the world is your oyster' were significant factors in its selection.'

I still prefer the holey oyster card story.

Pearly Kings and Queens

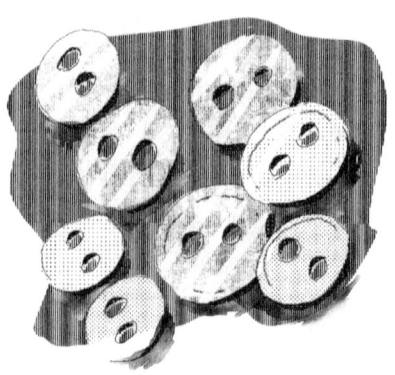

Mother of pearl buttons

The Pearly Kings and Queens are famous for wearing clothes decorated with mother-of-pearl buttons made from shells such as oysters and abalone. You might find iridescent shards of shells leftover from this button industry, discarded on the Thames foreshore. Henry Croft was the original Pearly King, and legend has it that he came across a load of pearl buttons on the Thames riverbank, sewed some onto his suit and cap and wore them out and about. Today there are Pearly Kings and Queens in different London Boroughs, each group is associated with a London church and committed to raising money for London-based charities. A parade of real-life Pearly Kings and Queens was featured in the London 2012 Summer Olympics Opening Ceremony, and there's a collection of Pearly King and Queen costumes and photographs at the Museum of London, Docklands.

Greenwich Pier Walk
From Greenwich Pier walking East and West to Deptford
   There are three aspects to this walk:-

1. East from Greenwich Pier
2. West to Deptford
3. Under the river by Greenwich Tunnel to the Isle of Dogs.

My Walk – South Bank walk from Greenwich Pier in both easterly and westerly directions
First, take a short walk from Greenwich Pier, east along the south side of the Thames foreshore, just enjoying the history of Greenwich and looking over to the huge O2 arena, Isle of Dogs and west to Canary Wharf and the City of London. Greenwich has popular historic sites to visit, such as the Royal Observatory, the National Maritime Museum and the Cutty Sark. Greenwich Palace was in Greenwich. At the end of the short easterly walk, turn around and head west, towards the City skyscrapers, and enter the old dockyards

and shipbuilding area of Deptford with its amazing industrial history. You can also walk under the Thames through the Greenwich Foot Tunnel to the Isle of Dogs and Canary Wharf. Recorded finds include a Mesolithic antler pick, a shard of Anglo-Saxon pottery, a ceramic chicken, maybe from the 17th century, and a rare fragment of a Raleigh clay pipe stem. Walter Raleigh introduced tobacco as a luxury item from Virginia in the 16th century.

My Walk from Greenwich Pier from East and West

Start
Catch the train to Greenwich station or take the Uber Boat to Greenwich.

1. Start to walk to the east, along the narrow part of the Thames Path, passing below The Old Royal Naval College. South of the College, you can see the hill of Greenwich Park with the Royal Observatory at the top.
2. Below the College, two sets of stone steps lead down to the foreshore, where you can walk along the sand and shingle. The bottom steps can be slippery with algae. Part of the foreshore at Greenwich, facing west, is now a Scheduled Ancient Monument because of the significance of the archaeological remains and the remains of the Tudor jetty or landing stage. You should not enter this part – see the Port of London Authority (PLA) map for details.
3. Walk east on the sandy foreshore towards The Trafalgar Tavern, built in 1837, with its elegant Regency river frontage and windows overlooking the water. The foreshore is more stony here and is littered with piles of bones in some areas.
4. Above you, just off the Thames Path, is Trinity Hospital, established in 1613, and there's a huge disused Greenwich Power Station by Crowley Wharf, where there are stone steps leading up from the foreshore with a handrail. Old

loading jetties for the Power Station loom above you. It was formerly an oil and coal-fired power station, but now it's been converted to gas and provides an emergency backup to power the London Underground in case of any disruption.

Thames Path

5. The shoreline here is tricky to negotiate with large granite stones, so it's best to climb up to the cobbled road by Ballast Quay, passing The Cutty Sark Pub, which serves tasty bar snacks. Follow the path northeast as it becomes Olympian Way, past modern blocks of apartments facing the river and planted reed beds until you find a new sandy area with access to the foreshore with a gate and steps down. There are excellent views over to the skyscrapers of Canary Wharf, the city and the Isle of Dogs that you can reach by walking through The Greenwich Foot Tunnel.

6. Return to Greenwich Pier along the Thames Path and link up with the westerly route to Deptford.

My river walk to Deptford

Deptford got its name from Deep Ford. It was here that pilgrims would ford the river on their way along the Roman Road to Canterbury, now the A2. Deptford was once the site of the East India Company, and the world's first commercial electricity plant opened in the vacant area in 1889. Plenty of water and coal was brought up the river to the landing stages on the riverbank to help power up Deptford Power Station, and you'll find lines of coal on the foreshore. Many new blocks of modern flats are being built, and many interesting architectural developments are going on in this area.

1. Just west of the entrance to the Greenwich Foot Tunnel, you get onto the foreshore at Billingsgate Dock steps down to the sandy shingle. At low tide, you can walk a short distance towards Deptford Creek along the shoreline.
2. Return to The Greenwich Foot Tunnel and walk west along the Thames Path, cross over the bridge at Deptford Creek, then twist along the pathways heading for Watergate Street. A narrow path runs down beside the Master Shipwright's House to the river by King's Stairs, also called St George's Stairs, with a handrail down.
3. Arrive on the narrow, shingly foreshore below the converted structures of Borthwick and Payne's Wharf. These stairs are the only exit point for this stretch of the foreshore, with Deptford Creek downstream and Deptford Strand upstream. The large metal walkways connecting the land above to the disused loading dock may be unsafe, so take care.
4. This is a spectacular foreshore in the centre of naval shipbuilding since the 15th century. Under Henry VIII,

it became the most important royal dockyard for the construction of warships. The river was deep in this area so that docks could be built, and Deptford was a hub of maritime and naval action in the middle of the 18th century. Over the centuries, famous captains such as Francis Drake, Walter Raleigh, James Cook, William Bligh and Horatio Nelson all sailed from Deptford.

In 1868, the area became a Foreign Cattle Market, with animals slaughtered on-site before they were moved. There are lots of old animal bones along this stretch of foreshore and plenty of chalk, which was laid down for barges to rest on so that they didn't get damaged by the sharp stones. Chalk was not naturally occurring in this area, and amongst the chalk are flints, including fossils such as corals and sea urchins.

5. Return up the King's Steps and make your way to Deptford Station, where you'll find plenty of coffee shops, bars and eateries under the arches.

The Greenwich Foot Tunnel to the Isle of Dogs

My walk
This walk takes you through the tunnel and then on a walk north east around part of the Isle of Dogs, with views overlooking The O2 arena. The Isle of Dogs is a tongue shaped piece of land jutting into the Thames opposite Deptford and Greenwich, with one side dominated by the skyscrapers of Canary Wharf.

The Greenwich Foot Tunnel is a red brick building with a green dome on top, and you can walk under the Thames from Greenwich to the Isle of Dogs in London. It opened in 1902 and was one of the City's most impressive engineering achievements. The tunnel was originally lined with 200,000 white tiles, but sections were replaced after the tunnel had bomb damage during the Second World War.

Over 4,000 people use this tunnel every day, and it will take 5-10 minutes to cross under the river. Sometimes, if the lifts don't work at either end of the tunnel, you need to climb the many stairs to get out.

It's free to use, and the Greenwich Foot Tunnel is open 24 hours, seven days a week.

Start
On the north side of the river, you have access to the river path around the Isle of Dogs, which was once a wild marshland area used for animal pastures and is now the financial hub of London. Some say the number of dead dogs that washed up on its banks gave the area its name, but it was called the Isle of Dykes or the Isle of Ducks. I did find part of a dog skull on the foreshore!

1. Exit the Greenwich Foot Tunnel and turn right through Island Gardens. Walk north east along the Thames Path NE Extension to Newcastle Draw Dock, which has access to the foreshore. At low tide, you can walk along below the Path, but watch out for the pinch points on the fast incoming tide. The foreshore has large bricks and stones in places, but it is sandy in parts.
2. An exit point from the foreshore is further along at Folly House Beach. There are exit ladders attached to the river wall.

Some pubs on the Isle of Dogs
The Ferry House dates back to 1722 and was the home of the ferryman who ran the free ferry to Greenwich.

The Gun is a historic pub and restaurant with a riverside terrace and views of The O2 arena. Built in 1790, Lord Nelson and Lady Hamilton had secret meetings in an upstairs room.

Did you know? Fun facts about the Greenwich Walk
Creekside Discovery Centre, Deptford
An educational charity running 'Low Tide Walks in the Creek'.

They kit you out to wade in the mud with an experienced guide who shows you the local and natural history of this amazing urban space. It's great fun and can be muddy. An interesting fact – the railway line bridge that crosses the Creek was too low for ships to enter to trade, so engineers designed the tall metal structure that you pass on the walk, which needed eight men to hoist up the rail track to give access for the boats.

The Cutty Sark is an award-winning visitor attraction by Greenwich Pier.
    The ship was the last of the great clipper ships and the fastest of its time. It used the wind to sail and bring goods such as tea from China and wool from Australia to London.
    On its first voyage, the ship departed London on 15 February 1870, bound for Shanghai with a cargo that included wine, spirits, beer and manufactured goods. After reaching China on 31 May, the ship was loaded with 1,305,812 lbs of tea, eventually arriving back in London on 13th October. Tea had been enjoyed in Asia for centuries, but it did not reach Britain until the 1650s when it was drunk for its medicinal properties and it didn't take long for tea to become a very popular British drink.

Mudlark with bucket

Nearly there

My Daft Mudlark Awards

After many days and occasional nights of mudlarking, as I discovered and recognised things on the foreshore, I awarded myself an imaginary Mudlarking Level 1 rosette. When working as the chief examiner for an exam board, I created marking systems with grades, so for a bit of fun, I've used that skill for Mudlarking.

Before you reach Mudlark Level 1, you'll mistake clam shells for the top of a clay pipe or get excited thinking that, at last, you've found a ring or coin. Sparkly shells look like silver treasure, and twigs can be mistaken for pins or pieces of buckle. When you identify and find the real items, you can move up a Mudlark Level.

Here is my analysis of Mudlarking Levels that I hope to achieve in the future.

Progression In Finding Clay Pipes

To help you understand my marking system, let's start with an example of Progression In Finding Clay Pipes.

As a novice mudlark, I wandered along the foreshore, spotted what looked like a white paper straw and picked it up to discover it was hard with a thin hole running down the middle. It was so exciting. I'd found my first broken piece of a clay pipe stem. Well done to me.

Now I'd got my eye in, it was time to find longer pipe stems and then move on to finding a pipe bowl. There's the progression in this search too. You may start with finding broken bits of pipe bowl, perhaps finding ones with a heel, then spot the decorated broken pieces.

You are on the way to achieving Mudlark Level 1, but on my award system, you can lose this status if you don't persist and go mudlarking in all weathers at all times of day and night.

You'll be tempted into online research about clay pipes and discover the famous drawings of English pipe bowls from 1580-1820 by Noel Hume. Notice how the drawing starts with really tiny bowls designed to hold small amounts of the expensive tobacco imported from the 1560s.

When you have collected a range of broken pipe bowls, you have reached Mudlark

Level 1 for clay pipes.

After the sixteenth century, tobacco smoking became very popular, and prices dropped, the pipe bowls got bigger and decorated pipes came into use to encourage more smoking.

To progress to Mudlark Level 2, you need to find an intact pipe bowl with a stem, and you'll rise towards Level 3 if you find an early pipe. Notice how the heels of pipes are labelled with the initials of the pipe maker and sometimes stamped with designs. Find the ends of stems that were dipped in coloured wax to stop the pipe stem from sticking to the smoker's lip.

Now, the challenge before progression for Level 3 is to find decorated pipe bowls. The clearer the decoration is carved in the mould, the higher the quality of the pipe. Pipe bowl designs with great stories imprinted into the design will elevate you towards Level 3. My best find was an elaborate pipe decorated with the word Egypt, an image of a castle, a sphynx and some royal feathers belonging to The Royal Inniskilling Fusiliers. It turns out the regiment served in Egypt between 1902 and 1908, so this pipe is old and has a story.

At Mudlark Level 3, you will find pipes with perfect bowls and stems, clearly decorated with elaborate mouldings such as faces, birds, figures, flowers and plants and some with dates and commemorations. The ultimate find is a whole Churchwarden pipe with an intact pipe bowl and a long stem up to 40 cm in length.

Now, to raise your Mudlark Level, you need to discover a range of other finds.

What about all the other river finds?
There's a progression in finding pottery sherds, glassware, coins, votive offerings, building materials, and metal stuff, but for details of each of these categories, you'll need to find an expert.

Mudlark Level 1 – You can spot and identify pipe stems and bowls, oyster shells, pieces of roof tiles, sherds of pottery and glass, glittery things and vapes.

Mudlark Level 1

Mudlark Level 2 – You strap on your knee pads and search the shingle to find pins, typeface, aglets and bits of buckles. Walking along, you find whole pipe bowls and stems, you can sometimes identify the age of sherds of pottery and their glazes, discover interesting shards from glass bottles, bits of Bellarmine jug face, Diwali offerings, and you imagine sharp pieces of flint are ancient Neolithic tools.

Mudlark Level 2

Mudlark Level 3 – On your searches on knees, you pick up garnets and beads with tweezers, find and identify coins, discover the top of a Tudor money pot, bits of wig curlers, musket and cannon balls, lead tokens, and much more. You start to take things back to the river that you no longer need, which gives joy to other newbie mudlarks. You may be able to help people identify finds.

Mudlark Level 3

Be aware that you can drop down from these levels if you stop mudlarking and finding things or get another hobby. And if you wonder, for now I've awarded myself Mudlark Level 2.

Only a few people carry on to reach the Olympic Mudlark Levels. They know who they are.

Olympic Mudlark Bronze Level – Finds pieces of pilgrim badges, discovers Roman coins, and valuable old and new gold rings.

Olympic Mudlark Silver Level – All the above but also finds a dead seahorse, very rare coins, specialist trade tokens, and rare badges with names on them.

Olympic Mudlark Gold Level – All the above but also finds a complete museum standard pilgrim badge, a hoard of old coins, a Roman carved god or goddess, a Neolithic flint axe head wanted by a famous museum, a rare named award badge.

More thoughts from mudlarks

Lisa Anderson has been writing her mudlarking blog since 2018, sharing her stories and research about her findings. @lizanderson2

'I'm a history graduate and former history teacher, a Londoner born and bred, of Polish heritage. History has been my passion for years, but until I started mudlarking, I knew little of Thames history itself – by that, I mean its archaeology, wharves, timbers and activity on it as a port for millennia.

Mudlarking finds are wonderful and teach us so much about the lives of forgotten Londoners from the past, but it's also important for me to record, photograph and map other Thames features – Saxon/Tudor fish traps, revetments, and old ships' windlasses before they're reclaimed by the Thames forever.

I love that mudlarking has given me a personal connection to the past, the handling of finds and the joy of sharing these stories with others.

Mudlarking is beneficial to my mental health, and that of others too, which I know from the many lovely comments to my blog from readers all around the world over the years, particularly during the stress of lockdown. I'm grateful for the friendships it's given me over the years, plus the kindness of other mudlarks who have shared their knowledge with me.'

Elle Harmer Instagram @ellerose_autumn_mudlarks

Elle is a passionate Thames mudlark who creates beautiful, artistic posts on Instagram and shares her finds from the foreshore at Isleworth, always supported by interesting stories of the objects she has rescued from the river.

'I love braving the foreshore in all weathers, discovering 'treasure', and learning the secrets of the past through research. One of my earliest memories is having Arthur Ransome's 'Swallows and Amazons' read to me. Another early memory is rifling through a skip near my grandparents' house. My brother and I were always taken on long walks and allowed to play outside. I think that if that sense of adventure and freedom to explore is nurtured, then it stays with you forever. I've heard people say that things like yoga had a transformative effect on them. That's how I feel about mudlarking. I can't imagine not being able to do it – it feels like part of who I am.'

Flora from Washed Up Cards

I joined Flora from Washed Up Cards on a jolly beach cleanup outside The OXO Tower one glorious summer's day. She runs group beach cleans, and creative workshops and makes handmade cards from the plastic and rubbish she collects from the riverbank. Visit her website and see how you can get involved. I guarantee you'll litter pick and laugh at the same time. Here Flora is called The Modern Mudlarker and explains why she loves her time by the river.

'I started going on litter picking walks during lockdown in our hour's exercise allowance and then made little greetings cards using some of the colourful plastic I had found washed up on the River Thames. I hoped my cards might help spread awareness about plastic pollution in a fun and engaging way. The social enterprise is called Washed Up Cards. Being outside and especially spending time closer to water doing things like beach cleaning massively helps with my mental health. I often say beach cleaning is like meditation. It's soothing for anxious minds because you have to concentrate and focus on a patch of sand and pebbles to find all the micro-plastic pieces. It's also a nice feeling knowing you're making a difference, however tiny, in the fight against plastic.

Washed Up Cards

I am a qualified River Action Leader with the charity Thames 21 and now run meditative beach cleans to get other people involved and feel the benefits I have experienced.'
https://washedupcards.uk

A final word from five year old Mia, who visited a riverbank for the first time with her mudlarking grannie.

'Mia what do you really like about going down to the riverbank?'

'It's so fascinating as you're by water and you don't know what you are going to find.'

'What did you find?'
'All sorts of shells, bits of glass, crabs, china, rocks, bone.'
'What sorts of bones?'
'A sheep's bone'
'Why do you think mudlarking is so popular?'
'I don't know.'
'Would you like to go again?'
'Yes please gran gran.'

Acknowledgements

My thanks to David Smith who accompanied me on the walks for this book and created all the artwork of the finds and river views. David has brightened up my textbooks with his amazing sketches for over thirty years and made my writing come to life, and his humour and criticism are much appreciated.

Thankyou to Jaime Rory Lucy, an expert mudlark, who has shared so much knowledge, checked the manuscript, and livens up our meetings by showing his fascinating findings of ancient artefacts that he brings out from his pockets like a magician.

To Jamie Mason and my sister Isobel who have encouraged me to write this guide, listened to my mudlarking stories and told me to get on with it.

Thankyou to the mudlarks who have inspired me and answered my question 'Why do you mudlark?' Many did not want to be named, as they quietly went about their hobby, enjoying the peace of the river environment and their history discoveries from the Thames.

Tobias Neto, a great mudlark who found the VC and has been a great teacher, showing me patience and skill as he searches the foreshore.

And to the special mudlarks who I meet down on the riverbank – Susan, Sahil, Wendy, Nat, Ben, Stephen, Sam, Daniel, Lukasz, Mike, Claire, Judy, Philly, Emma, Caroline, Sean, Sarah, Helen, Anna and so many more who have shared time with me, told me the stories of their finds and sometimes gifted me a treasure.

Thankyou to all the leaders who run the group tours along the foreshore – an incredibly, knowledgeable and diverse collection of people, entrenched in Thames history. I've enjoyed taking part in their tours – Thames Explorer Trust, Thames Discovery Programme, Thames Festival Trust and Thames21.

And thanks to my usual text editors Sue Goodchild and Eleanor Fox.

Lastly thanks to the many organisations that keep our river safe and patrol its waters. I often see their boats travelling up and down the river, checking things out and quite often surging through the water on a rescue mission. It is a comfort to know that when we mudlark they are only a phone call away. The Port of London Authority, London Fire Brigade, Coastguard, Thames River Police and Royal National Lifeboat Institute.

Printed in Great Britain
by Amazon